FOREVER
RIVALS

MONTREAL CANADIENS • TORONTO MAPLE LEAFS

FOREVER
RIVALS

MONTREAL CANADIENS • TORONTO MAPLE LEAFS

JAMES DUPLACEY • CHARLES WILKINS
EDITED BY DAN DIAMOND

Canadian Cataloguing in Publication Data

Duplacey, James
        Forever Rivals: Montreal Canadiens vs. Toronto Maple Leafs

Includes index.
ISBN: 0-679-30828-8

1. Montreal Canadiens (Hockey team) - History.
2. Toronto Maple Leafs (Hockey team) - History.
3. National Hockey League - History. I. Wilkins,
Charles. II. Diamond, Dan. III. Title.

GV848.M65D86 1996   796.962'648   C96-930866-3

Editor and Design: Dan Diamond
Photo Editor: Ralph Dinger
Captions: James Duplacey
Index: Eric Zweig
Coordinating Editor: Doug Pepper for Random House of Canada

Printed and bound in Canada on acid-free paper.

Random House of Canada
33 Yonge Street, Suite 210
Toronto, Ontario, Canada
M5E 1G4

96 97 98 99 00 01   1   2   3   4   5

" *There never has been, and never will be, an experience greater than a Toronto Maple Leaf and Montreal Canadiens hockey game."*

— Carl Brewer

" *Nothing else could touch the Leafs and Canadien rivalry. They both wanted to win so badly, and they gave it 100% game in and game out."*

— Dickie Moore

" *As a youngster in my house in suburban Montreal, my father was a fanatical Canadiens fan, so when I'd sneak upstairs to the bedroom to turn on the Maple Leafs game with Foster Hewitt, I'd have to keep it down low because I wasn't allowed to listen to the Maple Leafs."*

— Cliff Fletcher

" *Nothing could compare with the Montreal Canadiens – Toronto Maple Leaf rivalry. Hockey has missed that and hockey needs that rivalry again."*

— John Ferguson

" *There was an immense rivalry between Conn Smythe and Frank Selke, Sr. ... For (Smythe), beating the Canadiens, was like winning the war."*

— Bob Baun

" *As a young kid I was only taken to one game a year at the Forum. And it was always Toronto because that was the big game."*

— Ronald Corey

" *I think the rivalry started when Frank Selke was here in Toronto along with Dick Irvin ... They both left and went down to Montreal and of course they knew that Conn Smythe would develop a winner [back in Toronto] ... They wanted to build a club that would beat the Maple Leafs."*

— Sid Smith

" *Every time we went to Toronto, half the building was cheering for Montreal. And the same was true when the Leafs came to the Forum. I really believe the Leafs should have been in our division all the way."*

— Serge Savard

• • •

for our fathers,
H.D., R.D., L.J.D. and H.W.

• • •

FOREVER
RIVALS

...

CONTENTS

...

Carl Brewer (2) and Bob Pulford (16) combine to bring down Montreal's Claude Provost as Bob Baun (21), Pete Stemkowski (25), Red Berenson (2) and goaltender Terry Sawchuk look on. It often took two players to collar the pesky Provost, who was a premier defensive forward in the NHL during his 15-year career. In the 1964-65 season, however, he proved he could also contribute offensively. With both Jean Béliveau and Henri Richard nursing nagging injuries through much of the campaign, Provost was asked to supply some much-needed offense. The veteran responded by becoming only the fourth player since 1940 to lead the club in goals (27), assists (37) and points (64) in the same season.

The 1967 finals proved to be the last gasp of greatness for both Tim Horton (7) and goaltender Terry Sawchuk. While it's true that Horton would earn two more All-Star nominations, he would never reach the Stanley Cup finals again. Horton went to play for the New York Rangers, Pittsburgh and Buffalo before being killed when he lost control of his Pantera sports car returning to Buffalo after a game in Toronto on February 21, 1974. Sawchuk also roamed from team to team, but could never equal the success he reached with Detroit and Toronto. He also died tragically, succumbing to injuries suffered in an off-ice scuffle with teammate Ron Stewart in May, 1970.

I T WAS THE YEAR OF CANADA'S 100TH BIRTHDAY. The world's fair, *Expo 67,* was ablaze in Montreal, and from Newfoundland to Vancouver Island Canadians had kicked off their shoes for a year-long party. The NHL, like the country, was at a threshold. For nearly 25 years it had been a tiny paternalistic club, consisting of six teams, six owners and 120 players, who, with perhaps a few exceptions, were the best in the world.

The following season, the rich nostalgia and competitiveness embodied by those half-dozen warring tribes would be dissipated by an expansion that would push the league to 12 teams, and eventually to 26.

But in that last year, the grand finale for what many hockey fans still understand to be the "real" NHL — in that year of Canada's centenary — an unexpected cultural collision occurred that honoured not only the country and its sense of itself but also one of the brightest and most intense rivalries in the history of sport. The Toronto Maple Leafs and the Montreal Canadiens met in the Stanley Cup finals.

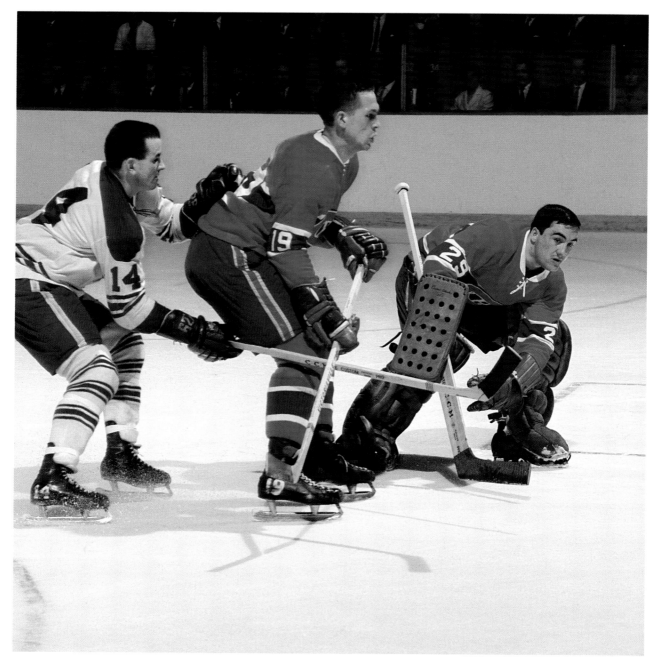

Dave Keon (14) pursues *Montreal rearguard Terry Harper (19) as Rogie Vachon clears the puck into the corner during the Centennial Year final. Keon's persistent pursuit of the puck and his relentless forechecking were two key facets in the Leafs surprising six-game victory over Montreal. His efforts were duly recognized when he was selected to be the third recipient—and only Maple Leaf winner—of the Conn Smythe Trophy.*

By any application of logic, it shouldn't have been that way. The Chicago Black Hawks were the best team that year, by a mile. In fact, with Hull, Mikita, Esposito, Hall, Pilote *et al*, they were probably the most compelling version of the club ever loosed on the league. As if by historic fate, however, an aging aggregation of Maple Leafs, catalyzed by the bounce and brilliance of a young Dave Keon, upturned the first-place favourites in the semi-finals, while the Canadiens were disposing of the fourth-place New York Rangers.

And so they faced off, the Habs in ascendance (they had won Cups twice during the past two seasons and would win eight more during the next dozen years), the geriatric Leafs about to limp from the stage that they had dominated throughout the early '60s (comedian Johnny Wayne would one day comment that they were the only team in the history of pro sport to have their dynasty ended by prostate problems).

With Chicago eliminated and the Leafs exhausted from their semi-final struggles, the Canadiens, despite finishing with their lowest point total in 14 years, had good reason to feel cocky about their chances of winning a third successive Cup; some said that they had champagne on ice at the Forum even before the series opened. Their line-up included six of the most talented Habs of the era — Jean Béliveau, Yvan Cournoyer, Henri Richard, Jacques Laperriere and Gump Worsley, future Hall-of-Famers all — as well as a support staff any member of which would have been welcome throughout the NHL: Dick Duff, John Ferguson, J.C. Tremblay, Ralph Backstrom, Bobby Rousseau, Gilles Tremblay, Claude Provost and Terry Harper.

It also included a rookie goaltender named Rogatien Vachon, who became an immediate focus of controversy when the Leafs' coach, manager and resident provocateur, Punch Imlach, declared to the press that the Habs "couldn't possibly win this series with a Junior B goaltender."

Imlach's pronouncement notwithstanding, the Habs won the first game 6-2. And might well have taken the second and third had the Leafs not settled into the doggedly defensive "non-style" that pretty much defined Imlach's brilliance as a strategist. Unlike his counterparts in Montreal (manager Sam Pollock and coach Toe Blake), Imlach had never been much interested in offensive flash or in "star" players — in fact he could barely tolerate the febrile likes of Carl Brewer and Frank Mahovlich, two of the most talented Leafs ever to wear the uniform. "What I want," he once said, "are guys who will play for *me*" — in other words, foot soldiers who would accept without question the stingy hard-working conformity that he perceived as the most direct and methodical means of winning. The true Imlach players Johnny Bower, Larry Hillman, Dave Keon, George Armstrong, Allan Stanley, Red Kelly, Bob Pulford and, of course, the ultimate Imlach archetype, Tim Horton, one of the most selflessly devoted Leafs ever. Throw a (barely) guided missile, Eddie Shack, into the mix and a handful of young players — Peter Stemkowski, Jim Pappin, Mike Walton, Ron Ellis — and you had the (somewhat motley) line-up with which Imlach hoped to defeat the defending Stanley Cup champions.

Asked after his resounding defeat in game one what he *now* thought his team's chances were of wresting the cup from the Habs, Punch smiled his cryptic world-weary smile (had he somehow foreseen the miracle that was to come?) and said, "Sure, we're down one, but with the guys I've got, it isn't gonna take any miracles."

As it turned out it did take a miracle — mostly of goaltending, but also of the savvy and Duracell forechecking of Dave Keon.

And of coaching, too. "Punch can be a hard man to work for," Tim Horton once said. "But if you do things his way you're going to win the Stanley Cup once in a while."

And that is what the Leafs did. Through five games their defencemen stood at the blue line, their wingers backchecked, and Dave Keon forechecked everything that came into his radar. The goaltenders, Sawchuk and Bower (who for more than two decades had suffered from debilitating arthritis), imitated teenaged contortionists in keeping the Habs at bay.

John Ferguson (22) and Yvan Cournoyer (12) celebrate Jean Béliveau's goal in game four of the Centennial Year finals. Although the Habs downed the Leafs with ease in this match, they couldn't penetrate the Leafs' stubborn defense for the rest of the series. When the Canadiens did get beyond the forechecking of Dave Keon and the bodychecking of Tim Horton, goaltender Terry Sawchuk was there to snuff out any scoring threat.

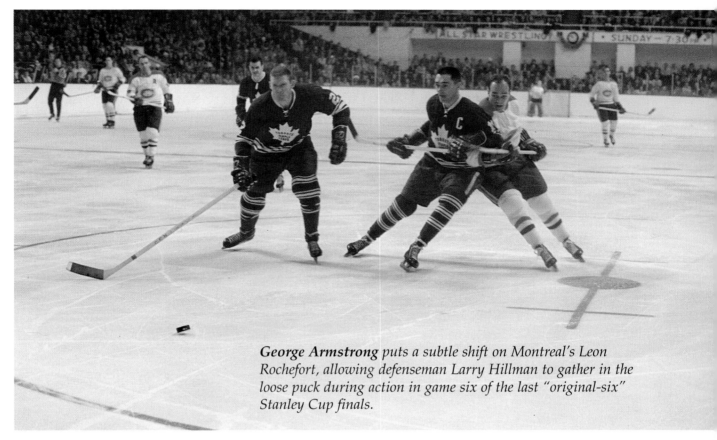

George Armstrong puts a subtle shift on Montreal's Leon Rochefort, allowing defenseman Larry Hillman to gather in the loose puck during action in game six of the last "original-six" Stanley Cup finals.

The Leafs held a 43-31 edge in shots in game two and parlayed goals by Stemkowski, Walton and Horton to a 3-0 shutout win. Game three required more than 28 minutes of overtime before Bob Pulford's overtime goal gave the Leafs a 3-2 win in a contest that saw the two teams combine for 116 shots on goal. The Canadiens bounced back to win the fourth game 6-2, then, perhaps overconfident, lost the crucial fifth game 4-1 on home ice.

The Leafs were within a victory of the championship as the series headed to Toronto for game six. By this time, Gump Worsley had replaced the "Junior B goaltender" in net, and Terry Sawchuk was making his stand in the absence of an injured Johnny Bower.

Throughout the first period of that final game, each goaltender was flawless. But during the second period, Ron Ellis and Jim Pappin beat Worsley to put the home team out in front. Ex-Leaf Dick Duff made the score 2-1 during the third and, as the minutes ticked down, fans of both teams, some eight million of them across the country, moved to the edges of their seats. With a minute to play, Montreal's coach Toe Blake called Worsley to the bench, leaving the Habs with an extra forward and an undefended net.

*Leaf defenders Allan Stanley (26)
and Tim Horton (7) try to slow down
the offensive surge of Bobby Rousseau
(15), Dick Duff (8) and Henri Richard
(16) during game six of the 1967
Stanley Cup finals. Duff managed to
break free of the Leafs' aggressive
checking early in the third period,
and zig-zagged through the entire
defense before slipping the puck
under Terry Sawchuk for the prettiest
goal of the championship final.*

"Boy, those were thrilling moments," said Leaf defenceman Allan Stanley in 1992. "At the final faceoff in our end, I was the last one over the boards when Punch called me back. He looked me in the eyes and said, 'You take the faceoff, Allan.' I gave him a second look, and he said, *'You take the faceoff!'*" (Believers in Imlach's mystical powers will swear that Stanley hadn't taken a faceoff in five or six years when Punch called upon him, but this isn't accurate. Like all defencemen, Stanley didn't take many draws, but he had lined up for a faceoff at least once in the Leafs' previous playoff series, a six-game semi-final victory over the Black Hawks. See accompanying photo.)

To some, Imlach's strategy might have seemed erratic, if not downright suicidal. But his reasoning seemed to be that a rangy, experienced defenceman like Stanley, then 41 years old, had as good a chance as anyone of tying up the Canadiens' brilliant centreman Jean Béliveau, who was accustomed to seeing and outwitting any number of others who might have come up against him at this pivotal point in the game (given his superstitions, Punch might also have felt that, on the endless scale of possibility, a guy named Stanley had a better chance than most of bringing home the Cup). Whatever his motives, he would *say* one day that he had assigned the job to Stanley because he figured an "old guy" would take longer to get out of position than a young one.

The forgotten faceoff. *Allan Stanley stands in against Phil Esposito in Toronto's semi-final series with Chicago. Note that Espo is clearly trying to gain an unfair advantage by lining up with his skates at an angle.*

"As I skated out to the circle I just kept thinking about what to do," continued the veteran defenceman. "Then I decided to do what our guys always did — take a swipe at the puck and a run at the opposing centre."

No Leafs fan of the era will forget the last tremulous seconds of the game. *"Imlach is making his stand with an all-veteran line-up!"* crowed Bill Hewitt above the bawling of the crowd. *"Stanley, Horton, Kelly, Pulford and Armstrong. Sawchuk, of course, is in goal."*

Referee John Ashley dropped the puck, and Stanley did what he had intended to do, managing in the process to pull the puck to Red Kelly, who kicked it to Pulford, who passed it to Armstrong heading up the wing. In his brittle, slow-motion style, Armstrong guided the puck toward centre ice and across the red line before wrenching loose his rheumatic-looking shot. Clocks stopped as the thing skipped across the Canadiens' blue line, the inside edge of the circle, the goal crease, and on into history.

Captain George Armstrong introduces the Stanley Cup to his teammates only moments after scoring the insurance goal in Toronto's 3-1 win over Montreal in game six of the 1967 finals. While it was the old-timers who provided the inspiration, it was the youthful threesome of Jim Pappin, Pete Stemkowski and Mike Walton who delivered the offense. The trio combined for eight goals and 18 points in the finals.

The size of the crowd was below expectations when George Armstrong and the Leafs paraded the Cup through the streets of downtown Toronto on an overcast day in May 1967. Perhaps the fans felt there would be many more opportunities to celebrate their good fortune. That, of course, has not been the case. Not only haven't the Leafs won another championship, no team in the history of the league has gone longer between appearances in the Stanley Cup finals then the Toronto Maple Leafs.

FOR CANADIAN FANS, the series had been a meeting made in the deepest recesses of their passion for the game of hockey. Since the years of the Great Depression, no sporting conflict had been more tantalizing to them or had thrown off such telling intimations of the nature of Canadian society than the one that existed between the Leafs and the Canadiens. To find a parallel athletic conflict, one would have to look to Scottish football, to the galvanic tension that has always existed between the Glasgow Celtics and Glasgow Rangers, preeminent symbols of Scottish Protestantism and Catholicism. In its heyday, the Canadian Football League offered a national debate between eastern and western Canada, manifested in the annual Grey Cup game. But for most of Canada, that rivalry was (by comparison to the Leafs-Habs epic) almost casually territorial and recreational, dependent not on commitment to specific teams and uniforms, but on the idea of east-versus-west and an annual party of exorbitant proportions.

Where the Leafs and Canadiens were concerned, the names of those who took the stage over the years were, alone, a Force-10 evocation of the intensity of the drama: Morenz, Joliat, Richard, Blake, Plante, Geoffrion, Béliveau ... Clancy, Conacher, Primeau, Jackson, Broda, Apps, Kennedy, Mahovlich, Bower, Keon. The stages themselves were iconographic symbols of the battle: the Forum in Montreal, Maple Leaf Gardens in Toronto. Throughout the '40s, '50s and '60s, at least 90% of Canadian fans sided with one or the other of the two teams (as Canadian kids of the era knew, table-hockey games came equipped with two teams only, out of deference to the overwhelming preferences of those who would be playing them).

The roots of the Toronto-Montreal rivalry went as deep as the defeat by the British of General Montcalm on the Plains of Abraham and the ensuing subjugation of the *habitants*, the common people of New France. (It is from *habitants* that the nickname "Habs" is derived.) The rivalry was tied up in an equally intense 19th- and 20th-century competition between the two cities in finance and business, and in the stiff English control of the NHL. Beyond that, the rivalry was stylistic, imagistic — part of a fundamental contrast between the cities (stolid Toronto, poetic Montreal) and, symbolically at least, the sharp divide between the

Albert "Babe" Siebert was one of those rare athletes who combined two outstanding careers into one. As a member of the arch-rival Montreal Maroons, Siebert was a slick-skating left-winger on the famed S-Line with Nels Stewart and Hooley Smith. Later, when his speed diminished, he became an outstanding stay-at-home defenseman with the Montreal Canadiens, winning the Hart Trophy in his first season with the club in 1936-37. He quickly endeared himself to the fans at the Forum, and he was a popular choice when he was named as the Canadiens' coach for the 1939-40 season. But before he could take his place behind the Habs' bench, he drowned in Lake Huron during a family outing. The third NHL All-Star Game was played as a benefit for his family.

sometimes pinched Presbyterianism of southern Ontario and the mysterious etherealness of the Roman Catholic Church in Quebec.

But the conflict was by no means *entirely* a polarity between French and English Canada. While the Leafs have enjoyed little support in Quebec over the years, both teams have long had hundreds of thousands of fans across the country. These days, when the Canadiens or Leafs show up in Calgary, Edmonton, Vancouver or Ottawa, the stands are alight with the visiting teams' traditional tri-colour or blue and white jerseys.

The surge of applause that invariably greets the Habs when they take to the ice in those cities would dumbfound Quebeckers who have come to believe that the rest of the country is one vast matrix of ill will and cynicism toward Quebec. In the days following the league's expansion to Vancouver, Calgary, Edmonton and Winnipeg, it was generally a visit from the Canadiens, with all that they represented of excellence and hockey tradition, that gave local fans a convincing sense of being a part of the larger picture. Moreover, the Canadiens' roster has typically contained a well-balanced mixture of French and non-French names. Some of the team's greatest stars have been anglophone: Siebert, Durnan, Lach, Blake, Harvey, Johnson, Moore, Worsley, Mahovlich, Gainey,

A lot of great hockey players played [in Montreal]. When you're playing with somebody that you think is better than you are, it makes you give something extra."

— Dickie Moore

During the six-team years *of the NHL, many players learned how to play through pain, because once you gave up your spot in the lineup, there was no guarantee you would get it back. Dickie Moore played the second half of the 1957-58 season with a broken wrist and still went on to win his first NHL scoring crown. Note that part of the palm of Moore's right glove has been removed. Many NHL players employed this scheme to get a better grip on their sticks and on their opponents. However, when defenseman Carl Brewer of the Leafs decided to remove the entire palm of his gloves, the league stepped in and made the equipment modification illegal.*

After the 1940 finals, *which the Leafs lost in six games to the Rangers, Conn Smythe, left, took a leave of absence from the team to serve in World War II. In the Smythe scheme of things, this also meant the end of the line for coach Dick Irvin, right, who according to Smythe, "wasn't tough enough, without me backing him up, to do what needed to be done. I wanted another man in there who would run the team the way I ran it." So Smythe offered Irvin to the last-place Montreal Canadiens and inserted Hap Day behind the Leaf bench. The move couldn't have worked better for both men. Day led the Leafs to five titles in ten years, while Irvin guided the Habs to the finals eight times, winning three championships.*

Dryden. The team's first superstar, Howie Morenz — "the Babe Ruth of hockey" — was born and raised near Stratford, Ontario.

It underscores the paradoxical nature of such thoughts to consider that, since the demise of the English-supported Montreal Maroons in 1938, anglophone Quebec has been all but unanimous in its support of the Canadiens. Indeed, over the past half-century, the Forum has been less a locus of political and social differences than a unifying place, where differences of language and culture have been sublimated to a greater cause, the pursuit of the Stanley Cup. When the Quebec Nordiques (now the Colorado Avalanche) became a charter member of the WHA in 1972 and joined the NHL in 1979, many hockey fans throughout the province of Quebec viewed them as an alternative to the Canadiens. The Nordiques — based just down the highway from Montreal in the French-speaking provincial capital — were positioned as a team of and for the *Quebecois*, the possessors of a kind of appealing rebel spirit. The unstated counterpoint was that the Habs represented "big-ness," the establishment, and that amalgam of anglophone and francophone interests unique to the city of Montreal.

Which isn't to say that the old fractures between the "solitudes" have not played a significant role in the Leafs-Habs drama. Leaf founder Conn Smythe, a one-time major in the Canadian army, who possessed little or no understanding of Quebec, hated French Canadians for, among other things, their resistance to joining the armed forces during World War II. He focused his hatred on the Canadiens, who he felt had stacked their war-time line-up with unenlisted players. He regularly called francophones "frogs" and on more than one occasion began speeches to public gatherings with the words, "Ladies, Gentlemen and Frenchmen." The war, however, was by no means the beginning of his bias against the Habs. During the mid-'30s, he had disgraced himself by engaging in a fist fight with the Canadiens' playing coach Sylvio Mantha, a fight that was ultimately broken up by Montreal owner Ernest Savard and league president Frank Calder. In 1938, during a game, he crossed the Forum ice in his street shoes to fight Savard himself.

But even Smythe's childish antipathies toward the Habs and French Canada were not unalloyed. In 1940, for example, when the Canadiens had finished last in the standings under coach Pit Lepine and were much in need of direction, Smythe phoned and offered them his coach Dick Irvin, who many believed was the best in hockey. "I guess what I did sounds strange," Smythe observed shortly before his death in 1980. "After all we'd been in the Stanley Cup final more often than not during Dick's years with the Leafs. But I was headed off to war and didn't think he was tough enough, without me backing him up, to do what needed to be done.... Montreal was delighted at the chance to get Dick, and he took a step up in pay." Smythe's comments were only slightly disingenuous. Irvin's departure opened the Leafs coaching job for highly regarded former captain Clarence "Hap" Day.

Smythe was far less sanguine about the abdication to Montreal in 1946 of his general manager Frank Selke, who had come to view Smythe as petty in his hockey judgements and demeaning in his relations with his employees. What few people knew at the time, or subsequently, was that the rift between Smythe and Selke began not as a clash of personalities or franchise loyalty but as a business matter — specifically, Smythe's request that Selke sell him his Maple Leaf Gardens shares, so that he could more easily assume

A bloodied but unbowed Maurice Richard *accepts congratulations from an equally bleary-eyed Jim Henry after the Canadiens eliminated the Bruins in game seven of the 1952 semi-finals. Moments earlier, Richard had blitzed his way through the entire Bruins team to score the winning goal, despite a head injury that had sidelined him for most of the game. While fans and scribes alike describe it as the greatest goal Richard ever scored, the Rocket remains mute about his historic moment. Knocked unconscious earlier in the same game, Richard doesn't recall anything about it.*

the presidency of the company after the war. Selke refused, then, seeing that Smythe would eventually become president anyway, resigned and went to Montreal.

Whatever his political, social or personal views, Smythe had no objection to having French-Canadian players or ex-Canadiens in his line-up if he considered them worthy of the privilege. Not that there ever *were* many, but in the years after his return from World War II he became obsessed in his desire to bring Rocket Richard, *l'idol d'un peuple*, to the Maple Leafs, whatever the cost (it is perhaps beyond coincidence that, in 1942, the Rocket had attempted to enlist in the Canadian army, only to be turned down because of hockey injuries). Smythe is said to have offered $100,000 to the Canadiens, plus players, and to have been prepared to pay the Rocket as much as $100,000 a season.

It redoubles the sense of shattered clichés to realize that Richard might have gone, had he not been so thoroughly indentured to the Canadiens. In an interview in 1989, he acknowledged that his foremost desire had always been to play in Montreal, but that he was embittered by the degree to which the teams of that era held dic-

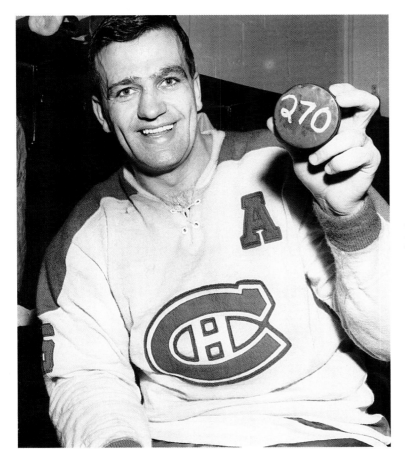

Bernie "Boom Boom" Geoffrion displays the puck he used to score his 270th career goal, tying him with Aurel Joliat on the Canadiens' all-time goal-scoring list. It was a special goal for another reason for Geoffrion. It also tied him with his late father-in-law, the immortal Howie Morenz, whose daughter he married in 1952. Later in the same game, a 6-2 victory over Toronto on December 7, 1960, Geoffrion fired home his 271st career goal to become the NHL's fifth all-time leading scorer.

tatorial control over their players. "Every year," he said at the time, "we'd go in and ask for a $2,000 raise, and they'd give us a thousand and tell us that we should be happy to be in the league. In the meantime, they were earning more money off us in a season than any of us could hope to make in a career. We should have been freer to move. At some point in my career, I'd like to have been able to earn what Smythe was offering."

At the time, the Canadiens' general manager, Frank Selke, opined that if he sold or traded Richard, he would expect fans to "tear down the Forum, brick by brick." If he had looked for a historical precedent, he might have noted that no such cataclysm had occurred when the team traded Howie Morenz to the Chicago Black Hawks in 1934. Then again, Morenz was anglophone. And Selke knew as well as anyone that it was the francophone names — Joliat, Richard, Béliveau, Geoffrion — and the exaggerated talents and achievements that went with them that had always

stirred the deepest emotions in francophone Quebec and brought the greatest sense of collective joy or despair. "For a very long time, the Canadiens were Quebec's only entree into North American sport," Toronto journalist Jeffrey Simpson wrote in celebrating the opening of the new Molson Centre in March 1996. "Tucked into a corner of the continent, speaking a different language and feeling sorely looked-down-upon by English-speakers, especially in the rest of Canada, the Canadiens showed vicariously what francophone Quebeckers could accomplish."

The Leafs, on the other hand, have always worn the symbol of the country squarely on their chests. Even during decades when much of Canada despised Toronto for its control of almost everything there was to control in the country, love for the Leafs was being seeded from coast to coast by the shrill voice of Foster Hewitt who, from 1931 well into the 1960s, made weekly national broadcasts of games from Maple Leaf Gardens in Toronto. "During the '30s, we'd gather around the radio every Saturday night," recalls Jack Warner, a retired farmer from Carlyle, Saskatchewan, who in 1993 fulfilled a life-long dream to attend a hockey game at Maple Leaf Gardens. "Even though we couldn't see what Foster was talking about, we seemed to know what it all looked like: the game, the building, the players. Oh, we loved the Maple Leafs!"

During the early years of the Toronto franchise, the names Conacher, Primeau, Clancy, Horner and Jackson were every bit as resonant to a prairie farm boy — to a kid *anywhere* in English Canada — as names such as Bennett, Roosevelt, Hitler, Churchill and Lindbergh. As the generations aged, new names took their place — on radio and then on television: Conacher gave way to Apps; to Kennedy and Sloan; to Mahovlich, Brewer, Bower and Keon. Journalist Trent Frayne once wrote that Hewitt's broadcasts brought together millions of Canadians "in living rooms and kitchens and bathtubs

FACING PAGE:
If there was any doubt *that Conn Smythe was an expert judge of both character and talent, it was put to rest when he put three young players together to form the "Kid Line." Charlie Conacher was a natural talent with a bullet shot who played the game with reckless abandon. "Gentleman" Joe Primeau was a master tactician who was always one step ahead of the play while Busher Jackson was a cocky, hardworking forechecker who was brilliant at working the puck out of the corners and could shoot and pass with equal efficiency. Together, they were a tightly knit unit that led the Maple Leafs to the Stanley Cup finals four times.*

Lorne "Gump" Worsley *had to overcome numerous trials and tribulations on his way to the Hockey Hall of Fame. Despite winning the Calder Trophy in 1952-53, Worsley was returned to the minors by the New York Rangers the following season. When he did get a reprieve, he had to endure constant criticism from coach Phil Watson, who didn't enjoy the Gumper's easy-going nature. Traded to Montreal in 1963, Worsley spent much of the 1963-64 and 1964-65 seasons in the minors or on the injury list. When he finally received his chance to shine, he ran with it, leading the Habs to four Stanley Cup titles. The pressure of playing in Montreal soon frayed his nerves and Worsley suffered a nervous breakdown during the 1969-70 season. He retired briefly, but agreed to return to the NHL after the Habs sold his contract to the Minnesota North Stars. He remained with the Stars until he retired in 1974 at the age of 45.*

and cars and on lonely dark farms and in small snow-packed towns and in big brightly lit cities from one ocean to the other" — all of them united in a kind of Maple Leaf Gardens of the imagination.

Beyond language and culture — but by no means divorced from either — the rivalry has of course been one of method, gamesmanship, playing style. From their earliest days as a franchise, the Canadiens have stressed flair and imagination, playing according to a strategic m.o. that is often referred to as "firewagon hockey": swift skating, agile puck skills, an appeal not just to the fans' most fundamental desire for conquest but for finesse and creativity. Which is not to say that flair has been pursued at the expense of winning (art matters little in sport if the home team is a loser). Rather, it was a *means* of winning, while simultaneously entertaining a city in which nobody — the fans, the press, the organization — has ever been satisfied with anything less than the Stanley Cup in spring.

So great is the pressure to play successfully in Montreal that it has at times overwhelmed players. Goaltender Gump Worsley ascribes his "nervous breakdown" in 1969, and his temporary retirement, to the relentless expectations of the Montreal press and fans. "We'd win a few and I'd be a hero," he said in 1990. "Then we'd lose a couple and people'd come up to me on the street and say, 'You lousy so-and-so; you don't deserve to wear the uniform.' You have to win in this city; there's no way you *can't* win and expect to survive."

"The fans in Montreal love you, win or tie," Hall-of-Famer Steve Shutt once joked.

The compulsion toward excellence exists not just on the ice but at every level of the Canadiens organization — from the training and weight rooms to the president's office. And its effects are amply illustrated by the team's extraordinary success: 24 Stanley Cups, compared to 13 for the Maple Leafs, and 33 for all other NHL teams combined. "Besides being the most successful athletic organization in the history of pro sport, the Canadiens are as well-managed businesswise as any corporation in North America," says Bobby Smith, who played with the team in the 1980s and has since earned a Master's degree in Business Administration from the University of Minnesota.

"When I was at business school we talked a lot about how a first-rate corporation will build up a kind of folklore around itself

One of Serge Savard's first major moves as g.m. of the Montreal Canadiens was to acquire Bobby Smith, the first player selected in the 1978 Amateur Draft and the league's rookie-of-the-year in 1978-79. Savard sent Keith Acton, Mark Napier and a draft choice to Minnesota to get Smith. Less than three years later, in 1986, Smith helped the Canadiens celebrate their first Stanley Cup win of the decade. He went on to lead the Canadiens in goals in 1986-87, and in assists and points in 1987-88 before returning to the North Stars to finish his distinguished career.

— Rolls Royce, Coca-Cola, whoever — and the Canadiens have done that so brilliantly. They've created this notion of the Canadiens as family, with ancestry, traditions, pride, responsibilities, all of that. And when you put on the uniform, you become part of it. And it's convincing. You believe in it. I mean, it's not just something somebody tells you about; it's in the record book; it was part of the building! Before the team moved, you could go into the Forum when it was empty and the lights were down, and you'd swear sometimes that the old voices and ghosts were right there with you."

In the Canadiens' dressing room, above the stalls, there have always been pictures of the great Hall-of-Famers of the organization — depicted in such a way that their eyes appear to be staring at the viewer no matter where the viewer is located in the room. "So you'd be putting your equipment on before a big game," says Smith, "and all the old greats would be looking right down at you, projecting this message that you'd better do your part. I remember

Bobby Clarke saying to me once that the Canadiens have an advantage over every other team. And they do — in this belief that they're special. For me, just to see the older guys coming around was a thrill: Dickie Moore, Jean Béliveau, Jacques Plante, occasionally the Rocket or Henri. Heck, it was a thrill just to be on the same ice as Guy Lafleur and Larry Robinson."

In Toronto, under Conn Smythe, who was involved with the team from the point at which he bought it in 1927 through the glory years of the six-team league, the desire to win was equally acute; indeed, it was codified to pretty much the extent it always has been in Montreal (it would not be an exaggeration to say that

A solid two-way center with a natural scoring touch and a fiery temper, Tod Sloan was one of the few bright spots for the Leafs during the dark days of the 1950s. A Second Team All-Star in 1955-56, Sloan led the Leafs in points and penalty minutes in 1954 and 1956. Sloan was the Leafs representative in the group who attempted to start a players' union during the 1957-58 season. Like many of the other "gang-leaders," he was dispatched to Chicago Black Hawks in June, 1958 when the union was squashed by the owners.

the *desire* to win is there still, although the Leafs have not reached the Stanley Cup finals since their last triumph in 1967).

But if the desire was equal, the approach to the game was not. Tactically, Smythe and his counterparts in Montreal were as different as the colours of the teams' respective uniforms: red from the feverish end of the spectrum, blue from the chill end. Few words in hockey lore have been as extensively quoted as Smythe's famous dictum: "If you can't beat 'em in the alley, you can't beat 'em on the ice." And that is the spirit in which he established his teams. While the Canadiens have always built around free-wheeling stars such as Morenz, Richard, Geoffrion and, later, Lafleur, Smythe built around character and toughness of a sort embodied by Charlie Conacher, King Clancy, Red Horner, Syl Apps, Gus Mortson, Bill Barilko, and Teeder Kennedy. Not that he was disinclined toward pure talent when he could get it (Conacher, Primeau and Jackson were immensely talented, as were Syl Apps, Tod Sloan and centre Max Bentley, who Smythe brought to the Leafs in 1947 to ensure the survival of the dynasty he had established during the mid '40s). But character came first; there were no prima donnas on Smythe's teams — no pandering, no indulgence of self-interest.

What there *was* on Smythe's team was passion. You couldn't play for him if you didn't have it. And there was an equal measure of it in Montreal. To survive in either town during the salad years of the six-team league, *you had to want to win* — more than anything else. And that meant commitment to good hockey. Beyond anything it might have represented in cultural or social terms, the rivalry between the Leafs and Canadiens was *about what happened when the puck was dropped and the game began*, about playing the game well. The intensity of the conflict honoured the brilliance, strategies and complexity of hockey. And, in so doing, it honoured the fans — *invented* many of them, providing and provoking the edgy anticipation with which the most devoted of them have always loved their sport. Inasmuch as Montreal and Toronto fans may have despised their vicarious rivals, in a very real sense they *loved* to despise them, knowing that their expectations for the game would have been sadly diminished in the absence of such beguilingly formidable enemies.

And so, once again, in the spring of 1967, the fans had been honoured in their allegiances and passions.

And in their hatreds, too, however cherished. Throughout the

Butch Bouchard and Rocket Richard head to the Canadiens dressing room after taking a post-game bow. When he retired in 1956, Bouchard handed the captain's mantle to Richard. That new responsibility, coupled with the calming influence of Toe Blake behind the bench, succeeded in mellowing the Rocket's rage without dampening his competitive fire.

'60s, the Canadiens and Leafs had played tough hockey, at times violent hockey. Their rivalry had *always* been fiery, had been marked not just by transgressions permitted within the rules, but by bitter feuding–much of which occurred well beyond the formal tolerances of the game. The annals of the conflict crawl with stories of violence perpetrated by the likes of "Red" Horner, the toughest of Leafs during the 1930s; "Wild" Bill Ezinicki, a Leaf enforcer during the mid- and late-'40s; Bill Barilko, Gus Mortson and Ted Kennedy, none of whom ever skated away from a scrap.

While the Canadiens relied less on pugnacity than on élan (during the '40s and '50s they took remarkably few penalties), their line-up, too, was perennially laced with players who would not brook a trespass or insult: Ken Reardon, Butch Bouchard, Bert Olmstead ... and, of course, Rocket Richard, whose legend as an agitator and pugilist is second only to his legend as a scorer. During the 1947 finals, for example, Richard committed what is perhaps the ultimate hockey malfeasance by smashing Bill Ezinicki in the face with his stick, drenching both Ezinicki and the ice with blood. An epic dust-up ensued, and during the teams' first game in Montreal the following season, Ezinicki boarded the Rocket so heavily that the gate to the Leafs' bench was knocked off its hinges. Ken Reardon and the Leafs' Vic Lynn met immediately

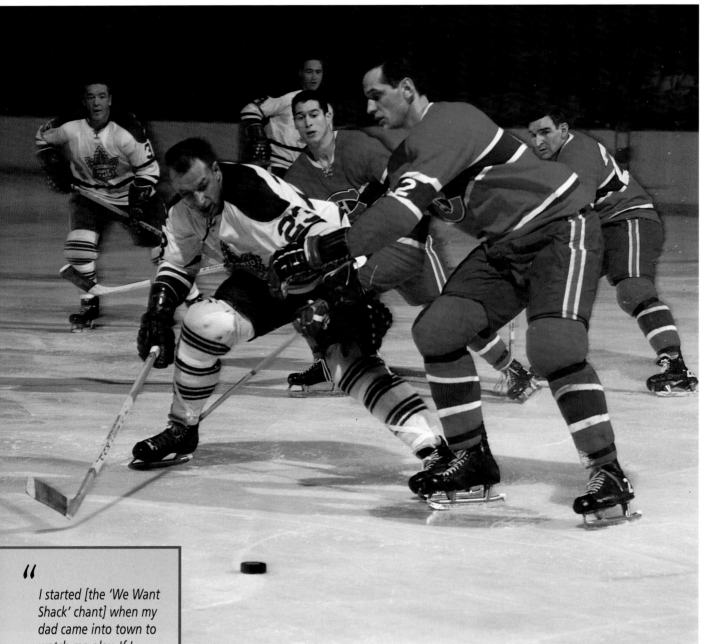

I started [the 'We Want Shack' chant] when my dad came into town to watch me play. If I didn't play in the first period, I'd say 'Dad, let's start "We Want Shack."' So he'd get the one side going and I'd get the other. Then Punch used to say, 'If they want you so bad, why don't you go up there and sit with them?'

— Eddie Shack

Eddie "The Entertainer" Shack *battles Montreal defenseman Jacques Laperriere for possession of a loose puck during the 1966 semi-finals as Hab enforcer John Ferguson (22) skirts along, just outside the action. Ferguson settled a personal vendetta against Shack and the Leafs by upsetting the forechecking of Pulford and Keon with bone-crunching bodychecks. Although the Leafs had an early lead in three of the four games, they ended up losing each match, thanks in large part to Ferguson's aggression. Fergy ended up outscoring, outhitting and outpunching Shack and the Leafs as the Habs won the series in four straight games.*

No player epitomized Conn Smythe's credo "if you can't beat 'em in the alley, you can't beat 'em on the ice" *more than "Wild" Bill Ezinicki. The Leafs' top cop on the beat from 1944 to 1950, Ezinicki was more than a one-way goon. He was a skilled athlete with quick hands, and he used them to score key goals and quick knockouts. After he retired in 1955, Ezinicki joined the professional golf tour and went on to win a pair of tournaments, including the Bob Hope Pro-Am.*

at the blueline and, for more than three minutes, wasted one another with what the *Globe and Mail* called "a non-stop volley of punches." The bloodletting perpetuated itself throughout the 1947-48 season and into the next when, in one game, referee King Clancy dispensed a league-record ten major penalties for fighting. And so it went.

The '50s were not years of utmost animosity between the teams, largely because the Leafs were not highly competitive through most of the decade. By the mid-'60s, however, hostilities had not only resumed but had been virtually reinvented by a pair of long-nosed, hard-headed sluggers: John Ferguson of the Habs and Eddie "Clear the Track" Shack of the Leafs. In the decades that have elapsed since, no Leaf or Canadien has come close to matching either of their reputations for ferocity. Which isn't to say there have not been other gladiators. Even during Ferguson's tenure, Montreal defenceman Ted Harris was as tough a customer as most clubs could have hoped to send into battle. And Tim Horton in Toronto is still remembered as the strongest player of his era, with the possible exception of Gordie Howe. "I remember being arrogant enough to take him on one night," says Derek Sanderson, an aggressive centreman with the Boston Bruins during the late '60s and early '70s. "I threw one punch, he put the bear-hug on me, and within seconds I was on the verge of passing out. It's not something I ever wanted to happen again."

Those who remember the '60s can still visualize Shack and Ferguson on the tips of their blades, flailing, hammering, tearing at one another, as the crowd howled its anguish or approval over a connected punch, a burst of fresh blood, a conclusive take-down. While Shack admitted in 1989 that he never really had much enthusiasm for fighting Ferguson, that he had done so largely because he felt it was expected of him, Ferguson acknowledges no such reservations about Shack — or about *any* Maple Leaf with

whom he exchanged hammerlocks during the eight years he was in the league (1963-71). "When I started with the Canadiens, I wanted to be the meanest, rottenest, most miserable cuss ever to play in the NHL," he said in December 1995. "I was so cocky, I just never believed I'd lose a fight to anybody. When Imlach was in Toronto, he'd often say he was bringing some guy up from the minors who was gonna do a number on me, and I'd skate by the Toronto bench, and I'd say, 'Who ya got this week, Punch? Send him out now!'"

Ferguson was an anomaly in the history of the Montreal organization, in that he was the first player brought to the roster specifically for his skills as a fighter. When he ascended from the American Hockey League, the Habs had not won a Cup in three years, having won five in a row during the late 1950s, and general manager Frank Selke felt the missing ingredient was toughness. Ferguson was, in fact, brought up specifically to derail the Leafs, who had won Cups two years in a row at that point. "Fergy was the most formidable player of the decade, if not in the Canadiens' history," says Jean Béliveau. "He'd do what he had to do to win, and he had to win; he wouldn't stand for anything less."

It is hardly a coincidence that after his arrival in Montreal in 1963, the Canadiens won Stanley Cups in four of the next six years. Nor is it a coincidence that in some fifteen years of junior and professional hockey, Ferguson was never traded (who in possession of such a weapon would put it in the arsenal of a rival army?).

On occasion, the Leafs and Canadiens *were* willing to trade assets into the hands of the enemy. But not often during the banner years of their conflict. It was not until 1981, in fact, that the teams conducted a mid-season trade. Of the trades that *were* made, there has been an almost disproportionate exchange of

FACING PAGE:
A supercharged John Ferguson (22) is carefully watched by Leaf blueliner Tim Horton (7) during the '67 finals. Ferguson first aroused NHL attention in 1962-63, when he scored 38 goals for the Cleveland Barons and led the AHL in penalty minutes. The Canadiens purchased his contract from Cleveland the following season and unleashed the hard-hitting Ferguson on the rest of unsuspecting NHL. It wasn't only his banging and belligerent attitude that made Ferguson unique. Throughout his career, he refused to fraternize with opposing players, both on and off the ice. He declined all golf tournament, hockey school and banquet invitations unless they were strictly all-Canadiens affairs.

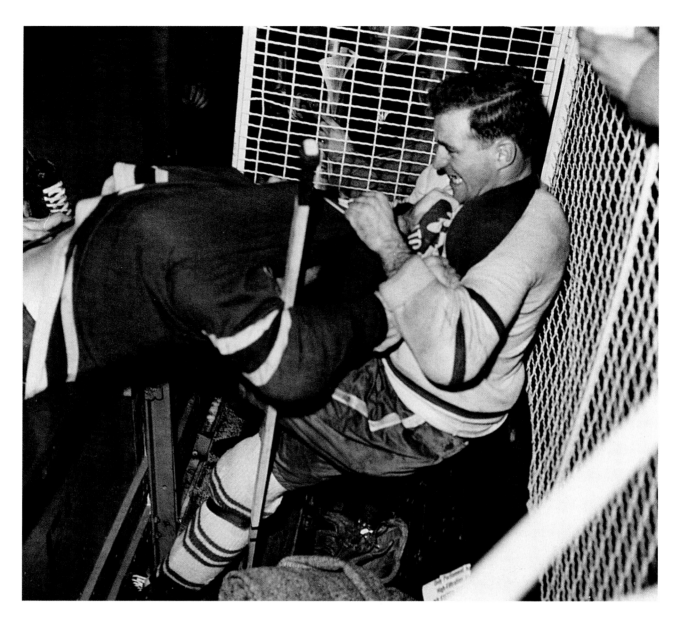

It may not be an alley, but the usually mild-mannered Dick Duff was more than willing to battle New York Ranger Irv Spencer from his seat in the penalty box. Duff began his NHL career as a Leaf before being traded to the Rangers in the deal that brought Andy Bathgate to Toronto. Midway through the 1964-65 season, the Rangers traded him to Montreal, making him one of a select group of players to play for both the Leafs and Habs.

goaltenders, starting with Lorne Chabot (Leafs to Habs) during the 1930s, Paul Bibeault (Habs to Leafs) during the '40s, and in later years, Bunny Larocque and Wayne Thomas, both of whom travelled from the Canadiens to the Leafs.

It is indicative of the competitiveness between franchises that only a handful of forwards and defencemen have ever moved directly from one club to the other. The most famous were Sprague Cleghorn, Bert Olmstead and Dickie Moore, and Moore's transfer in 1964 was not a trade or sale but a claim made by the Leafs in what was then the annual equalization draft. Moore had been retired for a full season when claimed by the Leafs. A number of influential players — Don Marshall, Ed Litzenberger, Dick Duff and Frank Mahovlich among them — have worn both uniforms, but none of them moved directly from one club to the other. Mahovlich, for instance, spent three years in Detroit between his years with the Leafs and Canadiens. Duff went from the Leafs to New York to Montreal.

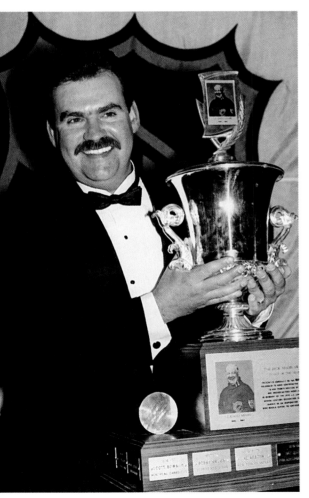

The only coach other than Dick Irvin to have patrolled both benches is Pat Burns, who moved from the Habs to the Leafs in 1992. While Irvin's move, in 1940, was sanctioned, indeed instigated, by his employers, the Leafs, Burns' move was unexpected and very much frowned upon by *his* employers in Montreal. Its net effect was to create a gleefully

Pat Burns became the first coach to win the Jack Adams Trophy with two different teams when he took home the award for leading the Toronto Maple Leafs back to respectability during the 1992-93 season. Burns, seen here accepting the award in 1989 when he was the coach of the Montreal Canadiens, kept the team moving forward until the 1995-96 season, when the players stopped listening, the team stopped winning and the fans started complaining. Like every other recipient of the Jack Adams Award before him, Burns was eventually relieved of his duties.

contemptuous satisfaction on the part of Leaf fans (who had seen their team steal precious little from the Habs in 30 years), as well as a hope that Burns might bring with him some of the discipline and desire that he had imparted to the Habs. Burns' tenure with the Leafs began positively — he was named coach of the year in 1993 — but within three years had disintegrated to the point where, in February 1996, he was ushered unceremoniously from the job, his team barely able to win a game, let alone a regular-season championship or a Stanley Cup.

Betweentimes, he brought the Leafs to the semi-finals two years in a row, and, in 1993, as close as they had come in 30 years to a berth in the Stanley Cup final. Had they got there that year, their opponents would have been none other than their old rivals from *la belle province*, who went on to win the Cup.

It is hardly surprising that hockey should have evolved in such dramatic fashion between the Leafs and Canadiens, given that the Canadian-style game was given gradual birth in an elongated cradle that stretched more or less between western Quebec and southern Ontario. As revealed in almost any text ever written about hockey, the game was played in primitive forms for centuries before it took root during the late 19th century in Canada. Certainly, a version of it was being played in Europe as early as the 16th century, and perhaps much earlier. One of the few pieces of empirical evidence of this is a painting, 'The Hunters,' by Peter Breugel, a Flemish artist whose career spanned the middle decades of the 1500s. In the foreground of the painting several hunters are trudging through snow, carrying their prey. In the distant valley below them, on a frozen river or canal, a number of tiny figures are clearly carrying what could only be described as hockey sticks. Their various poses indicate strongly that they are skating (primitive wooden and metal skates, perhaps like those used by the fabled Hans Brinker, are known to have existed in Holland as early as the Middle Ages). Because of the scale of the painting, it is impossible to see a puck, though the presence of the sticks is powerful evidence that *something* is being shoved around on the ice.

One might argue that the game being played in the painting is not hockey as we know it. In the same vein, neither was the game played in 19th-century Canada hockey as we know it. One of the first Canadian games on record, in 1875, was a crowded fracas played in Montreal by thirty McGill University students, all of whom were on the ice at once. Some wore skates, some street shoes. The game was played with a ball.

Up to that point, ice hockey, the rules of which were first set down in Montreal, had evolved among English-speaking immigrants as a conceptual alloy of several sports, including rugby, which gave the game its roughness and some of its regulations (initially, no forward passes were allowed); bandy, shinny and hurling, all of which were played with curved sticks; and lacrosse, which used goal posts and goalies. Winter provided ice...and plenty of incentive to keep moving.

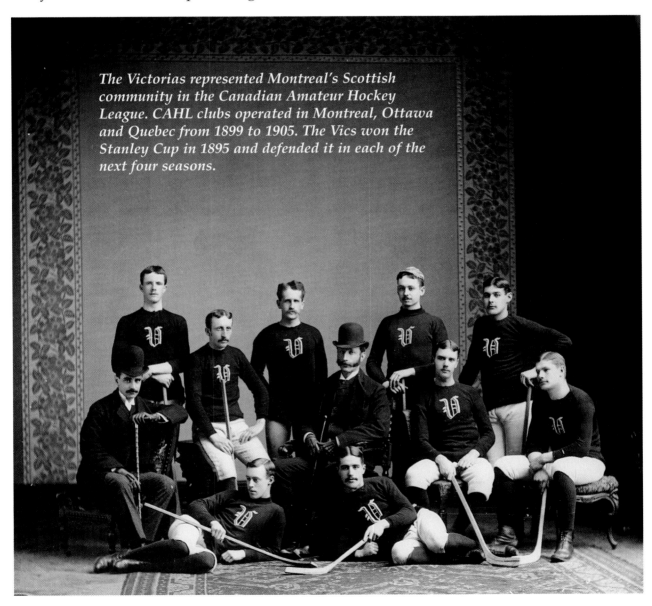

The Victorias represented Montreal's Scottish community in the Canadian Amateur Hockey League. CAHL clubs operated in Montreal, Ottawa and Quebec from 1899 to 1905. The Vics won the Stanley Cup in 1895 and defended it in each of the next four seasons.

It is a tribute to the burgeoning popularity of the sport that, by 1886, leagues had been formed in Montreal, and teams representing literally dozens of Montreal factions and immigrant communities were scouring the city for players. The Victorias, formed in 1880, were the main Scottish team, while the Montreal Amateur Athletic Association, formed in 1885, represented the English. In 1891, the Irish community formed The Shamrocks, which, along with lesser teams of Irish college students, became the first to introduce hockey to Montreal's other Roman Catholic community, the French-Canadians. For the young Frenchmen hockey was a conduit into the Anglo-Protestant world, which at that time virtually owned the game.

By 1898, however, two strong French-Canadian teams had formed, the Nationals and the Montagnards. They occasionally borrowed players from one another with the hope of defeating the best anglophone teams, but also engaged in bloody battles among themselves.

As teams and leagues emerged and dissolved in Montreal, hockey spread to Kingston (where a league was formed as early as the mid-1880s), to Toronto and to other parts of the country. But it was in Montreal that activity remained heaviest during the 1880s and '90s.

In 1893, the Montreal Amateur Athletic Association (MAAA) won the Dominion Hockey Challenge Cup, a trophy donated by Canada's Governor-General, Lord Stanley of Preston. Soon known as the Stanley Cup, this squat silver bowl was awarded to the top senior amateur team in the Dominion. During the first 11 years of the Cup's life, Montreal teams (Victorias, MAAA and Shamrocks) won it ten times.

In December 1903, the anglophone Montreal Wanderers were formed. The star-studded Wanderers were the first Montreal team to openly pay its players. Until then, "amateur" players had been paid with a few bills tucked discreetly into a pocket or the toe of a skate after each game. Although the Wanderers were defunct by 1918, they had a blazing career, defeat-

FACING PAGE:
By the 1915-16 season, *the Montreal Canadiens were wearing their now-familiar* bleu, blanc et rouge *colours. Led by future Hall-of-Fame members Newsy Lalonde, Didier Pitre, Georges Vezina and Jack Laviolette, the Canadiens defeated the Portland Rosebuds in a tightly contested five-game series to win their first Stanley Cup title. Goldie Prodgers, moved up to forward from his usual spot on the blue-line, scored the winning goal in the Habitants' 2-1 victory in the fifth and deciding game.*

ing eight opponents from Ontario, Nova Scotia, Manitoba and Alberta, in Stanley Cup challenges between 1906 and 1910 (the Cup by this time was accessible to professional teams).

But when the fully professional Canadian Hockey Association was formed in 1909, the Wanderers were rejected from its ranks, along with a team from Renfrew, Ontario, that had also hoped to be included. The snub, ironically, would be an unintended boon to the hockey world for nearly a century to come. For Jimmy Gardner of the Wanderers and Ambrose O'Brien, who represented the Renfrew team, would, in their umbrage, form a new league, the National Hockey Association, which would include not only the Wanderers, Renfrew and teams from a couple of other Ontario mining towns, but also a new team of the very best French-speaking players available — a team to be called the Montreal Canadiens. Well aware of the competitive power of ethnicity, O'Brien and Gardner felt the team would add a vital spark to competition and thereby attract larger crowds to games both in Montreal's east end and on the road in the north. Lest there be any doubt, the red, white and blue colours adopted for the team's jerseys in its second season were those of the flag of France, not the Union Jack.

By the NHA constitution, the Canadiens were the league's

French-only franchise — at least for the first three years. Before the 1912-13 season, however, the league relented to pressure and allowed the team to dress two English-speaking players. Other teams could sign two French players.

In 1916, under then-owner George Kendall (a.k.a. George Kennedy), the team won its first Stanley Cup. Its roster included a number of players — Didier Pitre, Georges Vezina, Jack Laviolette and Newsy Lalonde — who would eventually become franchise legends.

In 1917, the Canadiens became charter members of the brand new National Hockey League. When Kendall died in the flu epidemic of 1920, the franchise was bought by a brash trio of sports promoters that included Leo Dandurand, who would become the coach and manager and eventually be elected to the Hockey Hall of Fame. The new owners intended to sell hockey, both in Canada and the United States, and *les glorieux* were going to be their sales pitch.

At the time, the Canadiens played in the Mount Royal Arena, which seated 6,500 and was often packed for games. Construction of the Montreal Forum was completed in 1924 — for use not by the Canadiens but by a new NHL team, the anglophone Montreal Maroons. The rivalry was intense between the two franchises, but it was the Canadiens who won the Cup that year,

The Toronto St. Pats were residing in the Canadian Division basement when Conn Smythe and his investors purchased the team in February 1927. Smythe quickly went to work, molding the team in his image. He inserted himself behind the bench, shifted Hap Day back to defense and named him team captain and also signed American-born prospect Carl Voss. Five years later the team had a new home, a new image and a Stanley Cup champions

their first championship in the new league (they would win again in 1930 and 1931). The Maroons were strong athletically and they, too, won Cups in 1926 and 1935. But when they played the Canadiens at the Forum, French fans far outnumbered English, and by 1938, Maroon support had slipped to the point where they could no longer carry on. With the Maroons gone, the Canadiens became the Forum's sole NHL occupant. The arena would serve them well until 1996.

Of today's 26 NHL teams, the Canadiens and Leafs are the only franchises that date to the beginnings of the league. In 1917, the Leafs were called the Arenas, a team that had begun play in the old NHA under owner Eddie Livingstone, considered by many to be something of an "undesirable," for his low-life connections. Indeed, the NHL was formed specifically to get rid of Livingstone, who, just prior to the league's inaugural meetings (to which he was not invited), sold the team to new owners, who, in the NHL's first season, led it to the Stanley Cup.

Despite this on-ice success in 1917-18, the Arenas were in last place when they went out of business partway through the following season. The club was reorganized under new ownership for 1919-20 and, in the hope of attracting Toronto's burgeoning Irish community, was renamed the Toronto St. Patricks. But the attempt at an expanded audience failed, and the team drew poor crowds throughout the early 1920s. Toronto fans remained more interested in senior amateur hockey than in the professional game.

When the franchise went up for sale in 1926, a diminutive but strong-willed sports entrepreneur named Conn Smythe, who had once managed the New York Rangers, was galvanized to action. At the time, Smythe was managing and coaching the Varsity Grads, a team of University of Toronto alumnae, whom he had once coached at U. of T. and had led to the Allan Cup senior amateur final the previous year. He was a gambler, both in business and at the track, and, although he didn't have the resources to buy the team for the $200,000 asking price, he had $10,000 that he'd won betting on hockey and football games, and he was willing to stake his future on the probability of the team's success. He was quick to find investors and, having made the purchase, immediately changed the team's name to the Maple Leafs. "Our Olympic team had worn maple leaf crests on their chests in 1924," he wrote in his autobiography. "I had worn it on badges and insignia during the war. I thought it meant something across Canada, while St. Patricks didn't."

Smythe next decided that if pro hockey was going to grow in the city, his team would need a palatial arena in which to entertain its fans. He envisioned the place as a kind of Carnegie Hall for sport and imagined that, in such a setting, the game would become a premier attraction played not in front of slouches and rink rats, as was common for pro hockey at the time, but in front of a dressed-up crowd on its best behaviour.

The problem was that, by 1931, as his dream began to take shape, the Great Depression was tearing the heart out of the Canadian economy, so that, again, Smythe was short of money, although by no means short of nerve. Promising shares in the new endeavour to whoever would ante up funds, he was able to raise just enough start-up capital to begin. Inasmuch as he would one day harbour such vehement ill will toward Quebec, it seems ironic that during the spring of that year he went to a Montreal architectural firm, Ross & MacDonald, to have the Gardens designed, having been impressed by their work on Toronto's Union Station, Front Street Post Office and Royal York Hotel.

The land for the new facility, on the northwest corner of Church and Carlton streets, was acquired from the Eaton family, although not without difficulty. Initially, the Eatons believed that a hockey arena on the site would contaminate the atmosphere of their swank art deco department store located just a block west on College Street. Understandably, Smythe believed that to have the Eaton name connected to the franchise would help dispel pro hockey's slightly unsavoury image. And it is a testimony to his tenacity and salesmanship that the Eatons not only sold him the $350,000 parcel of land but also bought $35,000 worth of stock in his enterprise. The sporting conflicts that would eventually transpire on the property had a fitting historic precedent. During the Rebellion of 1837, William Lyon Mackenzie's insurgents had met the local sheriff and his men in a decisive battle on precisely the site of the present-day Gardens.

On June 1, 1931, construction began, just five months before the facility would be needed for the upcoming hockey season. To offset shortages of capital, Smythe paid tradesmen up to 25% of their wages in Gardens shares. However, few of the 1,300 workers involved held on to the shares. Most sold them immediately back to Smythe who is said to have paid them for the certificates with a commodity far more comprehensible to the average construction worker — cartons of cigarettes.

As a further cost-cutting measure, Smythe eliminated a pair of balconies that had been included in the original plans and reduced the number of windows. He once said, "I had to scrounge, beg and borrow, everything but steal, in order to keep the project going."

In 1988, King Clancy, a star Leaf player of the day, recalled being "overwhelmed" on visiting the half-finished building "because it was so much bigger than anything I'd ever seen. I wondered where they'd ever find people to fill all those seats." (As originally configured, the Gardens held 12,473. Today, its capacity is 15,746.)

As the building neared completion that autumn, the newspapers hailed its construction as a "miracle," both of speed and financial wizardry. And they reveled in the details of the construction: 750,000 bricks, 77,500 bags of cement, 1,200 tons of gravel, a million board feet of lumber, 540 kegs of nails, 230,000 concrete blocks. The time clock above centre ice — installed for the 1932-33 season — weighed five tons.

The Gardens was officially opened on November 12, 1931, and, in the months that followed, Foster Hewitt's dramatic play-calling proved irresistible to a population suffering the stresses and deprivations of the Depression. "Our little world was brightened by those broadcasts," recalled journalist Dick Beddoes in 1981. "They were money from home at a time when there was no money at home or anywhere else. We didn't know how rich we were to be so well entertained on Saturday nights."

Although the Maple Leafs lost their first game in the new building, they did win the Stanley Cup that year, strengthening their grip on the hopes and imaginations of millions of fans across the country.

Meanwhile, in Montreal, the Canadiens had become a kind of devotional focus for French Canada, or at least for French Montreal. By 1931 they had finished either first or second in the NHL's Canadian division for five years straight, and had won Stanley Cups in 1930 and '31. Although they would not meet the Leafs in a Stanley Cup final until 1945, the rivalry between the two had been intense since 1920 — at times savage. Players such as Billy Coutu, Sprague and Odie Cleghorn of the Canadiens thought nothing of slashing, spearing or butt-ending an opponent — or simply just beating on him with their fists, until he was unconscious.

Odie once claimed to have participated in "more than 50 stretcher-case fights," and in 1983 Sprague was described by Leaf great King Clancy as "the dirtiest, meanest, most vicious man" ever to have knocked Clancy cold. "He was a master of the butt-end, could bust your jaw, take your teeth out, fracture your ribs. And he was a great stick handler, too."

The Toronto stars of the early '20s included the likes of Jack Adams, Reg Noble and Babe Dye, who won scoring titles in 1923 and '25 and finished no lower than fourth in scoring for five con-

Cecil "Babe" Dye captured headlines for the St. Pats in Toronto while Howie Morenz was doing the same thing for the Canadiens in Montreal. An outstanding baseball player who spurned numerous offers to turn pro, Dye was the NHL's deadliest sniper throughout the 1920s. Dye, who led the league in scoring in 1922-23 and 1923-24, also played an indirect role in the formation of the Toronto Maple Leafs. When Conn Smythe was assembling the New York Rangers, the club's owners wanted him to acquire Dye as a marquee name for the newly formed franchise. Smythe, knowing that Dye's skills were wearing down and his weight was going up, refused to make the deal. When the new Chicago team grabbed Dye, Smythe was given his walking papers and Lester Patrick was brought in to run the Rangers. Later, Smythe used the "golden handshake" money he received from New York to purchase the St. Pats and rename them the Maple Leafs.

Dubbed the "Stratford Streak,"
Howie Morenz was hockey's marquee
star during the pro game's early years of
growth in the United States, keeping
tills full and turnstiles clicking during
the worst years of the Depression.
Morenz was the complete package. He
could skate, shoot, pass and, when the
occasion called for it, fight better than
anyone wearing skates at the time. With
this combination of speed, stamina and
smarts, Morenz blazed a Hall-of-Fame
trail that saw him become the first
three-time winner of the Hart Trophy as
the NHL's most valuable player.

> "
> (Morenz) was a
> hurtling forward. He
> had so much speed and
> he was so light on his
> skates. You just feel
> when he was coming
> down the ice, that ...
> his blades would only
> hit the ice about every
> third stride. He was just
> so fast, such a great
> stick handler ... And a
> terrific competitor,
> too."
>
> — Red Horner

secutive seasons between 1921 and 1925.

But no Toronto player of the era could match the star quality of a young man from southwestern Ontario named Howarth W. Morenz, who joined the Canadiens in 1923 and played his last game early in 1937, a little over a month before his death. Morenz appealed to the fans in a way that no other player had before, and was a major force, perhaps *the* major force, in convincing American promoters that hockey was not merely a sport for the frigid cities of the north, but a big-league attraction for the American metropolis. During Morenz's career, the NHL grew from four Canadian teams (struggling to survive) to an international circuit that, at times, encompassed as many as ten franchises. Montreal journalist Andy O'Brien, who covered the Canadiens during Morenz's career, once compared him to a compact version of Bobby Hull. "He would challenge the opposing defences by dazzling dash and deception," said O'Brien. "You didn't have to know anything about hockey to be lifted from your seat by Morenz — just as you didn't have to know anything about baseball to be thrilled by a towering home run by Babe Ruth."

"He was the best I played against, and the best I've ever seen," said King Clancy. "He could get to top speed in one stride, he was a threat to go from end to end through an entire team at any time and he shot the puck as hard as any man who ever played."

Toward the end of his career, Morenz played briefly for the Black Hawks and Rangers, but returned to the Canadiens for a final season in 1936-37. It is one of the enduring mysteries of sport that some six weeks after this powerful young man broke his leg on Forum ice on January 28, 1937, he was dead — apparently of related causes. What is known is that a great deal of drinking and partying went on in Morenz's hospital room as he convalesced. Certainly, any number of clichés have been applied to his passing: "His great heart stopped"; "His will to live was gone"; "He died of a broken heart." And he may indeed have succumbed to some sort of heart attack or stroke. But rumours have never been entirely dispelled that when the cast was removed, it was ghastly evident that the whole leg had become gangrenous, black, and that in his despair Morenz took his own life.

Whatever the case, the day after his death his body was placed in a coffin at centre ice of the Forum, where thousands of people filed past to pay their respects. Fourteen thousand turned out for his funeral, and another 200,000 are said to have jammed the streets to watch his cortege as it rolled toward Mount Royal Cemetery.

As Morenz's fame had reached its zenith in Montreal during the early '30s, Toronto's adulation had fallen increasingly on a trio of Leaf youngsters who to this day retain storied identity as "The Kid Line": Joe Primeau, Harvey "Busher" Jackson, and Charlie Conacher. Primeau, a rare paragon of non-violence for any Smythe-run team ("Gentleman Joe" he was often called), was the centre, the playmaker, while Jackson and Conacher provided speed and goal-scoring on the left and right wings. Conacher had both strength and moves, and is credited by some with being the first to use the slapshot. But he and Jackson were carousers, drinkers, womanizers; Conn Smythe once described them as "too busy driving their new cars and chasing women to bother getting in shape." During the Depression, Conacher and his brother Lionel ran a bootlegging operation above a Toronto garage. And by the time Jackson was traded from Toronto to the New York Americans in 1939 his drinking was the stuff of local legend.

And it cost the team. While the Leafs made it to the finals six times during the '30s, they won only one Cup, in 1932, and would not win again until '42. However, if current judgement is unkind to Conacher and Jackson, the record book is not. Conacher led the league in goal-scoring five times during the mid-'30s, and Jackson finished his career with 241 goals, a total surpassed only by Nels Stewart's 324, Joliat's 270 and Morenz's 270 among players of that era.

Moreover, if the Leafs of the day couldn't win in the finals, the Canadiens were far worse. They didn't even *get* to the finals between 1932 and 1944, by far the dreariest period in the history of the franchise. Four times in succession during the late '30s and early '40s the club finished either last or second to last in the seven-team league. Which isn't to say that these years were entirely lost to either club. During the late '30s in Toronto and the early

Walter "Turkey Eyes" Broda was originally the property of the Detroit Red Wings, but Conn Smythe was able to "steal" him for his Maple Leafs team. Broda was playing for a Detroit farm club in Windsor, Ontario, when Smythe spotted him. The Wings were strong in goal at the time, so they sold Broda to the Leafs for $8,000. He went on to become one of the game's greatest "money" goalies.

Conn Smythe was an astute judge of talent, both on and off the ice. He first spotted Syl Apps during a football game between McMaster University and the University of Toronto that was held as a warmup to the 1934 Grey Cup match. Apps, playing halfback for the McMaster side, was unstoppable and had carved out a large chunk of yardage by the mid-game whistle. Smythe had been told by Art Ross that the kid was planning to enter the ministry and was probably too soft to be a pro player. That was incentive enough for Smythe. He found a telephone at halftime and used it to add Apps' name to the Leafs' negotiation list. Three years later, Apps was rookie-of-the-year and well on his way to becoming one of the greatest players to ever wear the Maple Leaf.

'40s in Montreal, a rejuvenation took place that would lead eventually to the most successful dynasties that either franchise has ever produced, and to one of the most competitive periods in their famous rivalry.

In Toronto, the process began in 1936 with the acquisition of three players. Corpulent goaltender Walter "Turk" Broda would prove to be the best the Leafs had ever had. He was a "money" goaltender, whose lifetime regular-season goals-against average was just over 2.50, but whose playoff average was 1.98. Up front, the Leafs added a clean-living, clean-playing university graduate named Syl Apps and a big right winger named Gordie Drillon. No less a witness than Teeder Kennedy calls Apps one of the two greatest players he ever saw (the other is Gordie Howe). "People who played with him or against him knew how great he was," says Kennedy. "He could take the puck and roll with it. He was a great skater, he could score goals. He'd make things happen. There weren't all that many players in the league who could make things happen. Syl was one." The following season, 1937-38, the two young Leaf forwards worked magic. Centred by Apps, Drillon collected 52 points in 48 games to win the scoring championship with Apps finishing just two points back.

Of equal importance was the ascendancy of former player Hap Day into the head coach's job in 1940, after Dick Irvin was dispatched to Montreal. Day was conservative but crafty and, unlike Irvin, quickly developed a reputation for being able to win the big games. In 1942, with players such as Billy Taylor and Sweeney Schriner in the line-up, he led the Leafs to the second Stanley Cup of their 16-year history.

Two years earlier, at the outbreak of World War II, Conn Smythe had written letters to all Leaf players urging them to do their duty and to enlist in the Canadian armed forces. And most of them took training while they were still with the team. Smythe himself would eventually form the famous Sportsmen's Battalion, a group that included a variety of athletes and sports writers but no hockey players. The unit saw action in 1944 at Caen, France, where Smythe suffered such serious wounds to his leg and internal organs that, initially, there was doubt he would survive.

Shortly after the Stanley Cup victory of 1942, heavy call-ups began, and, as the conflict progressed, the heart of the Leaf team — including Apps and Broda — went off to war. The result was that for the next two years the team lost in the first round of the playoffs.

Even so, good things continued to happen for the Leafs. They acquired "Babe" Pratt, a walloping defenceman, from the New York Rangers, and, in 1943, Theodore "Teeder" Kennedy, a fearless, play-making workaholic, who, as he matured, would lead the team to a decade of success unparalleled in its history. It is an ironic footnote to the Toronto-Montreal rivalry that Kennedy could never have become a Maple Leaf had it not been for the cooperation of the Canadiens, who, unbeknownst to him, had put the young man on their "negotiation list" as a teenager and owned his playing rights. When it came time for the Habs to try to sign him, however, the Port Colborne, Ontario, teenager wanted nothing to do with them; he had grown up listening to Foster Hewitt and couldn't countenance playing for any other team than Toronto. It is doubly ironic that Kennedy would become a particular nemesis

of the Canadiens, and that the man who acquired him for the Leafs, Frank Selke (defenceman Frank Eddols was sent to Montreal in return) would eventually become manager of the Canadiens and would deeply regret that he had ever made the move. "Kennedy always killed us," Selke once said. "It was by far the worst trade I ever made."

Smythe, who was overseas at the time, was furious to hear that Eddols, a top prospect, had been traded away without his permission, particularly for an unknown (whom he would eventually herald as "the greatest Leaf of them all"). Selke would later admit that making the trade without obtaining Smythe's okay was a breach of club discipline, but was sure that the deal was a sound one. This incident created a rift between the major and his general manager that never was resolved.

In the meantime, in Montreal, coach Dick Irvin had rejuvenated a team of bottomfeeders and had embarked on a course that, between 1944 and '47, would see the team finish first in the standings four times in a row and win two Stanley Cups, in 1944 and '46.

The defensive heart of the team in those days was a massive French-Canadian country boy named Emile "Butch" Bouchard, who broke in in 1941 and would be with the team until 1956. The goaltender, Bill Durnan, was a Toronto native who won the Vezina trophy during his first season as a pro (1943-44) and repeated as winner in six of the next seven seasons (the Leafs' Broda won the other time). But the visceral measure of the team could best be taken from a line of forwards that featured the somewhat fractious Elmer Lach at centre, crafty "Toe" Blake on left wing and, on right wing, the man

FACING PAGE:
Ted Kennedy was the hardest working player *to ever skate in Maple Leaf Gardens. Because he was neither stylish nor graceful, he had to labour for every inch of progress he made on the ice. Kennedy, with his face straining and his legs pumping, made every fan in the building appreciate the effort he was putting out. His presence created a tradition that remained a fixture at Leaf games long after Kennedy had hung up the blades. Whenever the team was struggling, some leather-lunged fan in the cheap seats would rise and bellow "C'mon Teeeee-ddder," and the entire arena would respond with a thundering roar that gave even the most disinterested fan a spine-tingling shiver.*

who in 1945, three years after he broke in, emerged as the identifying icon of the organization, an honour he retains to this day: Maurice "Rocket" Richard.

Richard is thought by many to be the most spirited professional that hockey has ever known — and the game's finest scorer. In an era when scoring 20 goals a season was considered a mark of excellence, he several times scored more than twice that many and, once, during the 1944-45 season, scored 50 in 50 games, a

Bill Durnan was a Toronto native who had no intention of playing in the NHL. But the Montreal Canadiens convinced the ambidextrous goalie to try the professional game and he immediately became the sport's dominant netminder. One of the keys to Durnan's success was his unique style of switching his goal stick from hand to hand, depending on which side of the ice the action was unfolding. By constantly changing hands, Durnan could confuse his opponents and always have his catching hand protecting the wide side of the net.

record that stood for 37 years. But it wasn't just the *number* of goals that the Rocket scored; it was the way he scored them. Hall-of-Fame goaltender Frank "Mister Zero" Brimsek once said, "He could shoot from any angle. You could play him for a shot to the upper corner and he'd wheel around and fire a backhander to the near, lower part of the net." Another Hall-of-Famer, goaltender Glen Hall, said of the Rocket, "When he skated in on net, his eyes would shine like a pair of searchlights. It was awesome to see him coming at you."

To be sure, it was the Rocket's eyes that signalled the spirit within. Even in publicity shots his eyes burned with an animal passion — the Rocket's Red Glare, it has been called. During the early 1950s, American novelist William Faulkner, on special assignment for *Sports Illustrated* magazine, went to Madison Square Garden to watch a game between the New York Rangers and the Canadiens. A short time later he wrote that one player, Richard, had stood out beyond the others with the "passionate, glittering, fatal, alien quality of snakes."

Commenting on the potency of the Rocket's personality, Frank Selke once said that even when the Rocket wasn't playing, the sheer force of his personality could lift the team. "All he had to do was to be in the dressing room or on the bench. Nobody dared clown around when he was there. He came to win, and the others

Most of Rocket Richard's *scoring records have been surpassed in the modern era of longer seasons, increased scoring and four rounds of playoffs, but no NHL player can match Richard's record of six overtime goals in the Stanley Cup playoffs. Richard scored once in extra time in 1946, three times in 1951 and once in both 1957 and 1958.*

caught the spirit from him. No one could take liberties with our team when he was there, and opposing players knew it."

In the spring of 1945, the Leafs, many of whose best players were still in Europe, placed third in league standings, barely above the .500 mark, while the Canadiens, led by Richard's phenomenal 50 goals, finished way out in front with 80 points in 50 games. Before the teams met in the semi-finals, Montreal coach Dick Irvin declared that his team was "the greatest of all time." It was a gauntlet that hardly needed to have been thrown down. For in the years since the beginning of the war, the Toronto-Montreal rivalry had escalated from sporadic hostilities to the most bitter confrontation in hockey. The conflict was, in part, about the bitterness that had developed between French and English Canada over the ease with which francophone Quebeckers had been able to get

Coach Hap Day addresses the troops at the opening of training camp in 1944. Despite the absence of many key performers, including Syl Apps, Turk Broda, Gaye Stewart and Bud Poile, the Leafs went on to win the Stanley Cup. In the semi-finals, the Leafs faced the Montreal Canadiens for the second consecutive season. Day's squad avenged its previous playoff loss to the Habs by downing Montreal in six games thanks to the offensive output of Ted Kennedy and the scintillating goaltending of rookie Frank McCool.

Elmer Lach from Nokomis, Saskatchewan, joined the Canadiens as a 22-year-old rookie in 1940-41. He was originally scouted by the Leafs, who brought the youngster east to play for St. Michael's College, the crown jewel of the Leafs' farm system. Lach wasn't ready for the big city and he quickly hightailed it back home, without telling Conn Smythe or the Leafs. Canny Conn never forgave Lach for the slight and traded his rights to the NY Rangers. When Lach refused to report to New York, the Broadway Blues released him. Paul Haynes suggested that the Habs take a chance on the playmaking centre and Lach went on to play his entire career with Montreal. On February 23, 1952, Lach became the NHL's all-time leading scorer, a title he held until teammate Rocket Richard wrested the crown from him on December 12, 1953.

deferment from joining the services. It was also about Dick Irvin coaching the team that had dismissed him and about the egregious ill will that existed, for example, between Ted Kennedy of the Leafs and the Habs' Elmer Lach.

Kennedy's winger, Bob Davidson, recalls Lach saying to Kennedy early in the series, "You come near me and I'll take your head off with my stick," and Kennedy growling back, "You try it and I'll put you in the bloody hospital." According to Davidson, the veteran Canadien would "run" most centremen in the league. But when he tried it on Kennedy, the young Leaf "would bring his stick up, right in Lach's face. You could not scare Teeder one iota."

It is a tale on the order of David and Goliath that, with his skills and attitude, Kennedy, then only 19, was able to singlehandedly derail the Canadiens' great line in that 1945 series, permitting the Leafs to defeat the Habs and then go on to win the Stanley Cup over Detroit.

By this time, the Canadians and Leafs had settled into a pattern of league domination that would see them combine to take a remarkable 28 of 38 championships between 1942 and 1979.

Nevertheless, the following year the Leafs, even with their returned veterans, failed to make the playoffs. Kennedy had been debilitated for most of the year with a groin injury, but Smythe laid much of the blame for the fiasco at the feet of his manager Frank Selke. For this and for reasons outlined earlier, Selke quit the organization and signed on as managing director of the

> **"**
>
> *When [Teeder Kennedy] took his first faceoff against Elmer Lach, the puck dropped and Lach's stick came up and carved up his face. And Lach just said, 'Welcome to the league, kid.'*
>
> — Sid Smith

Canadiens, which further heightened tensions between the clubs.

With the humiliation of the previous season fresh in mind, Smythe and his coach Hap Day proceeded to rebuild the team around players such as Broda, Apps, Kennedy, Howie Meeker and four of the game's toughest, hardest-hitting defencemen: Garth Boesch, Bill Barilko, Gus Mortson and Jim Thompson. A teammate once said of Mortson, "He wasn't big, but if you went into the corner with him and came out with the puck, he'd take your ankles off." The same player said of Bill Barilko: "If he got a piece of you, you hurt for a week. He just tore you apart."

Understandably, the Rocket was a favourite target of the foursome during the late '40s and is said at times to have "exploded" with fury after being decked by Barilko or Boesch. Today, he acknowledges that his temper was "too fast," that he did not have the necessary self-control to turn his back on provocation. He says, "If I took a bad bodycheck, I had to retaliate, had to go after the guy right away — and I took a lot in games with the Leafs; they were the dirtiest team in the league at that time. And I never mellowed, even in the end."

Richard's quarrel with the Maple Leafs extended well into his retirement: "One night in the mid-'60s," he recalls, "a Leaf defenceman, Kent Douglas, hit Bobby Rousseau over the head

A quartet of Leaf goal-scorers (left to right: Vic Lynn, Gus Mortson, Ted Kennedy and Bud Poile) celebrate Toronto's 4-2 win over Montreal in game three of the 1947 Stanley Cup finals. Lynn is brandishing a nasty war wound that he received during an encounter with Rocket Richard in game two of the series. Richard, who was given a match penalty in that game, was suspended for game three because of his stickwork on Lynn and Leaf enforcer Bill Ezinicki.

with his stick. I was sitting just above the passageway the players go through on their way to the dressing room at the Forum. When Douglas passed underneath I tried to hit him on the head with my fist."

Frank Selke frequently reiterated his star's assessment of the Maple Leafs of the late '40s, speaking out loudly against their "dirty clutch and grab" style of play.

The Canadiens defeated Boston to win the Cup in 1946, but the following year, 1946-47, the strength of the rebuilt Leafs kicked in, setting up the first Leafs-Habs final in NHL history.

The character of that landmark series evolved along a frantic competitive axis that enjoined not only the teams' great stars, Richard and Kennedy, but the goaltenders, Turk Broda and Bill Durnan (during the last three games each team scored just five goals in total).

It was a brutal affair, the battle lines for which had been drawn six weeks earlier when the Leafs' Nick Metz had bodychecked Elmer Lach so aggressively that Lach's skull had been fractured, sidelining him for the year. As the series opened, coach Dick Irvin is said to have implored his team to "win it for Elmer" — presumably at any cost. Richard's barbaric slashing of Vic Lynn and Bill Ezinicki (in the face) during the second game — a violation that earned Richard a one-game suspension — pretty much defined the tone of the six-game contest.

In the end, the Leafs were left standing — as they would be the next year, and the next, making them the first NHL club to win three successive Stanley Cups...the league's first so-called dynasty.

The teams met again for the Cup in 1951, in a series that has acquired almost totemic significance in hockey lore — largely because all of its five games went into overtime, but also because of the famous photograph that shows the Leafs' Bill Barilko diving iceward as he scores in overtime of the fifth game to end the series. The photo's grip on successive generations of viewers lies not just in the spectacle of the image, or the awareness that the Cup was won at precisely that moment, but in the morbid knowledge that the Leaf hero flew north on a fishing trip three months after the photo was snapped and was never seen again. Rumours filled the newspapers about his disappearance, the most bizarre being that he was a Russian spy who had defected across the North Pole to his ancestral homeland.

Bill "bashin' but never bashful" Barilko gives a one-fisted salute after scoring the Cup-winner in 1951. A free-spirited defenseman, Barilko loved to join in the play in the offensive end, a strategy that coach Joe Primeau strongly discouraged. Before the start of the 1951 playoffs, Primeau called Barilko onto the carpet and warned him to "stay-at-home" on the blueline. After he had scored the Cup-winning goal, Barilko skated right to Primeau and said, "Joe, you didn't want a hook that time to keep me back there, did you?"

So reluctant were the Leafs to accept Barilko's loss that when the 1951-52 season opened six months later, Barilko's equipment was placed dutifully in his stall in the locker room, with the expectation that he might somehow materialize and reclaim it.

For the Canadiens, the early '50s were a significant threshold. A number of key players, including Doug Harvey, Butch Bouchard and the Rocket, had been with the team for some time, but the addition of players such as Bernie Geoffrion (1950), Dickie Moore (1951), Jacques Plante (1952), and Jean Béliveau (1953) created a unit that, within five years, would be the greatest dynasty the league had ever seen. Béliveau's signing was undoubtedly the most significant. In the years that led up to it, he had been playing senior hockey for the Quebec Aces, under Punch Imlach, and had become such a crucial part of the scene in Quebec that in order to keep him in the city the Aces management was willing to pay him anything offered by the Canadiens, who owned his professional rights and desperately wanted him in their line-up. Quebec's protectiveness was partly a concern for keeping good hockey in the city but also for paying off the mortgage on the publicly owned Colisée, which had just been built and which Béliveau, with his extraordinary talents, was capable of filling night after night.

For three years prior to joining the Habs, Béliveau came to their training camp, only to return to Quebec. During the 1952-53 season, after a three-game trial in which he scored five goals and inflamed the hopes of the Montreal fans, Selke offered him a $53,000 contract: $20,000 to sign, then three years at $10,000, $11,000 and $12,000 a year. The only Canadien making money even close to those amounts at that time was the Rocket himself.

Béliveau turned the offer down.

In the end, Selke, always a man of imagination, came up with a solution: the Canadiens would buy the Quebec Senior League and turn it into a professional league, thereby forcing Béliveau to honour his "professional" responsibilities to Montreal. And that is what they did.

In October 1953, in front of television cameras, Béliveau signed a five-year contract worth $110,000, including signing and bonus clauses. When Selke was asked how he had convinced his new star to sign, he said, "It was really simple. All I did was open the Forum vault and say, 'Help yourself, Jean.'"

In the years since, another take on the signing (or *delay* in signing) has come to light. It has been said that during 1950 or '51, representatives of the Quebec government, concerned over the debt

After his remarkable junior career with the Quebec Citadelles, Jean Béliveau decided *to sign with the Quebec Aces of the QSHL instead of joining the Montreal Canadiens. His coach with the Aces was Punch Imlach, who is seen here discussing strategy with Béliveau in the Quebec dressing room. Béliveau won a pair of scoring titles with the Aces before finally signing with the Canadiens in 1953.*

on the new Colisée, contacted Frank Selke and let it be known that if Béliveau was signed before the debt was under control, the province would have the Forum closed down for fire code violations. Selke is said to have retorted that if the government was willing to risk losing the vote of every Habs fan in the province, which was to say 90% of the population, they should go ahead and do it.

The tale is apocryphal, although the Forum was indeed a decrepit, substandard arena until a significant renovation took place in the summer of 1968. Even at its most dilapidated, the Forum — along with Maple Leaf Gardens — perennially represented the highest ideals and respective mythologies of the home team. For Canadiens players, the Forum was known respectfully as *la maison*. "It wasn't my second home," one-time captain Yvan Cournoyer said in 1995, "it was my first. I was more comfortable there than anywhere else on earth. Most of the guys felt that way." For the team's fans it was a dream world — a palatial repository of memories and desires. And the Gardens possessed the same powerful ethos. "For decades, even in the middle of summer, people have come from all over the country just to take a look at the place," says Don McKenzie, who fought in Conn Smythe's Sportsmen's Battalion and, from 1946 to 1990, was the Gardens' building superintendent. "I used to show lots of them around inside, and as they'd get out into the seating area I'd notice that a kind of reverence would come over them, and they'd get quiet, and I'd see them staring up into the rafters as if they were in a cathedral or something."

Dr. Leith Douglas, who for nearly three decades has been the Leafs' plastic surgeon, says that in spite of his familiarity with the Gardens, it still "feels like a temple" to him. "I like to be there in the evenings when there's nothing going on, no one's around, and the lights are down. At times like that, I can hear all these voices from the past talking to me: Punch Imlach, Turk Broda, King Clancy, Foster Hewitt..."

The '50s were not great years at the Gardens, as the Leafs slipped into decline. But the Forum was never more exciting. The Canadiens defeated Boston for the Cup in 1953, the last championship for coach Dick Irvin, then, beginning in 1956, under coach Toe Blake, went on a tear that would bring them five successive Cup championships, a record that still stands. In 1955-56 they finished with a record 100 points, 24 points ahead of the Red Wings, who had supplanted Toronto as their main competition. The team's line-up included four of the league's top seven scorers — Béliveau, the Rocket, Bert Olmstead and Geoffrion — plus a pair of youngsters, Henri Richard and Dickie Moore, who, within a couple of years, would themselves figure prominently in the scoring lists. To fans of the era, particularly Leaf fans, the Habs seemed (and indeed proved to be) invincible. They had more talented forwards than any two teams in the league combined, and a defence corps led by the incomparable Doug Harvey whose effortless "rocking chair" style — a combination of strategic intelligence and extraordinary skills — controlled not just opposition attacks but, seemingly, the entire pace of a game. What's more, they had the brilliant and innovative Jacques Plante in goal — the first to wear the mask, the first to wander the ice in the vicinity of the net and

The on-ice accomplishments of Doug Harvey have been well documented—seven Norris Trophy wins and ten First All-Star Team nominations. But he was also an award-winning athlete off the ice. Not only did he play Double-A pro baseball with Ottawa and win the league batting title, he also starred as both a running back and defensive back with the Montreal Alouettes of the Quebec Rugby Football Union, which later became part of the Canadian Football League.

to be involved in the play. Plante was a poet at his position and, in many ways, a polestar for the creative spirit of the team.

From a political perspective, the hockey of the '50s in Montreal is best remembered for the so-called "Richard Riots" of 1955. *Globe and Mail* columnist Lysianne Gagnon recently called the riots "the beginning of Quebec's Quiet Revolution" in that they marked a first public outcry by Quebeckers against the perceived domination of Quebec culture by non-francophones — in this case control over the fate of Richard and the Habs by the English administration and interests of the NHL. The impetus for that outcry was league president Clarence Campbell's decision to suspend Richard for the entire playoffs because he had walloped a referee in a late-season game against Boston. The Canadiens, who were facing a life-and-death playoff battle with rival Detroit, could hardly win without their star forward and motivational heart. "They could have suspended me for ten, fifteen games the next season," says Richard. "I would have accepted that. But not the playoffs! Oh, I was mad."

Canadiens supporters were equally incensed by Campbell's decree. When the team returned to the Forum for its next game, Campbell, who regularly attended the Canadiens' home games, entered the arena and took his seat, ignoring a sustained assault of insults, boos, and projectiles. He had been warned by both the police and the mayor not to attend the game. At the end of the first period, with Detroit leading 4-1, a fan threw a smoke bomb that landed within yards of Campbell's feet. Montreal's fire marshal ordered the building cleared. The game was forfeited to Detroit, who leapfrogged the Habs in the standings. The Red Wings, who would also defeat the Canadiens 6-0 in the last game of the season, would finish in first place, two points ahead of Montreal.

In the aftermath, thousands of angry fans poured from the Forum and raged down Ste. Catherine Street, throwing rocks,

FACING PAGE:
After piloting the Toronto St. Mike's juniors *to a pair of Memorial Cup titles, Joe Primeau moved behind the bench of the Toronto Marlboros and led the senior team to the Allan Cup title in 1950. The Senior Marlies club included future Leaf captain George Armstrong (front row, far left), future Leaf owner Harold Ballard (front row, third from left) and future Leaf coach John McLellan (front row, second from right).*

breaking store windows, destroying whatever lay in their path.

"We didn't win the Stanley Cup that year," says Richard, "and I didn't get my playoff money. But we did win the Cup the next five years in a row, which kind of helped me forget about losing it in '55."

A LARGE PART OF THE HABS' SUCCESS in the '50s lay in the blossoming of a vast farm system started by Selke during the late 1940s to ensure the team's ongoing success. By the mid-'50s, the club controlled more than 10,000 amateur players on 750 teams, mostly in Quebec and in the talent-rich prairie provinces. There were ten Canadiens farm clubs in Winnipeg alone; a whole amateur system in Regina; another in Edmonton, the latter consuming some $300,000 a year in expenditures. The Habs also sponsored minor-league *professional* teams in the American Hockey League, the Western Hockey League and, of course, the Quebec Professional Hockey League.

Toronto, too, had a vast and productive farm system during the '40s, '50s and '60s, mostly in Ontario, but also among the minor professional leagues in cities such as Rochester, N.Y., Tulsa, Pittsburgh and Victoria, B.C. The system was so strong during the early '60s that it was sometimes said the Leafs' main AHL team, the Rochester Americans, had as many major-league-calibre players as some of the lesser NHL teams. The same was true of

Montreal's system, which routinely graduated players onto the rosters of NHL teams that either refused to or could not afford to spend money on feeder systems of their own.

"I operated those minor league clubs like a farmer," Selke once said, "nurturing good potential players like plants and helping them come up and ripen in the system until they were ready to join the big club." From 1950 on, Selke's right-hand man in running the farm system was a young Montrealer named Sam Pollock, who would eventually take over as general manager of the team, running it with the same shrewd judgement and integrity that he had studied in the man who had hired him.

Selke and Pollock were chiefly responsible for giving the organization its paternalistic dimensions — the aura of familial empathy on which it continues to pride itself. Pollock, for example, instituted a practice of giving honoured players a year's salary upon their retirement. What was asked of those players was that they, in turn, honoured the club by retiring "with dignity," instead of, say, complaining about being "pushed" or reeling off to join some other team. If a player could be persuaded to go quietly, the impression of *la famille heureuse* was preserved. In many cases, former stars and lesser players found post-hockey career prospects greatly enhanced in Montreal by their status as valued Habs alumnae.

Perhaps needless to say, this studied family atmosphere has not always produced harmony between the club and its "sons." Some of the greatest of the team's players have left the organization severely disaffected. For twenty years after his retirement, the Rocket harboured a nagging grievance over the fact that Selke had forced him too early into retirement. An outraged Bernie Geoffrion severed ties two years after retiring, when the club reneged on a promise to make him coach. Guy Lafleur left under a cloud after feeling diminished by the duties of the front office job the club had asked him to perform. More recently, Patrick Roy disavowed his role as a favourite son.

The Leafs, by comparison, alienated *dozens* of players over the years. During the Imlach and Ballard years, they distanced perhaps more players than they managed to keep loyal: Mahovlich, Brewer, Bathgate, Keon, Palmateer, Sittler, MacDonald, Tiger Williams, Turnbull... The list is long, although some of those spurned have more recently returned to the fold.

Even under Conn Smythe, players and employees were not

always happy. Frank Selke is a good example. So, too, is Eric Nesterenko, a Leaf prospect of the early '50s who Smythe believed would one day be another Jean Béliveau. "I guess ultimately I disappointed the old man," says Nesterenko. "But I don't care. He was an exploitative old son-of-a-bitch. I had no use for him. Eventually, I got into a big fight with the Leafs about how they were playing me. In those days you didn't question ownership or management at all, and in 1956 they got rid of me, sold my rights to Chicago."

In 1958, the Leaf organization (control of which had by now fallen to John Bassett, Harold Ballard, and Conn Smythe's son Stafford) hired an obscure, mule-driving manager named Punch Imlach, who they believed could restore the team's lost glory. But halfway through the 1958-59 season, the Leafs had done little to convince their fans that they had forsaken their long-held lease on

When he first arrived on the scene in 1952, Eric Nesterenko was compared to Jean Béliveau, a billing he could never live up to. Nesterenko could never fit into the limited mold the Leafs had built for him, and he left the team to return to university midway through the 1955-56 season. Sold to Chicago in the off-season, he continued to pursue his college degree while playing only weekend games with the Hawks. In 1957-58, he returned to the NHL full-time and became one of the league's best two-way forwards during his 16-season stay with the Black Hawks.

the league crawl space. Then in early December, Imlach fired his coach Billy Reay and established himself behind the bench, repeatedly promising anyone who would listen that his team would be present when the playdowns for the Cup began. "My guys are gonna rise up like Lazarus," he told a caucus of reporters in early January 1959. "In fact, if Lazarus isn't under contract, I might like to sign him for the stretch run." The sportswriters and fans loved it. They'd endured seven years of a team that founder Conn Smythe had compared to jellyfish, and even the *prediction* of a playoff spot was more exciting, and made better press, than no playoffs at all.

And, sure enough, during the last few weeks of that "Cinderella" year, the Leafs began to stir, then rise precipitously. The record shows that between March 14 and March 22, they won four games in a row, climbing from seven points back of a playoff spot to within a point of the swooning fourth-place New York Rangers. On the last night of the season, still one point out of a playoff spot, they wheeled into Detroit for a fateful game with the Red Wings who had recently replaced them at the bottom of the NHL food chain. Behind 2-0 at the end of the first period, and with owner co-owner Stafford Smythe gloomily allowing that the season was over (between periods, he went so far as to congratulate Punch on "a pretty good year"), the team quickened to prophetic impulse. By the end of the second period they had tied the game 4-4.

By the time they left Motown that night, they had a 6-4 victory in their pockets and were a playoff team, as promised.

Sixteen days later, they finished off the Boston Bruins in the semi-final, before conceding the five-game final to the unbeatable Canadiens.

Imlach had inherited a talented group of young players, the cream of the Toronto junior program: Bob Pulford, Dick Duff, George Armstrong, Billy Harris, Bob Baun, Ron Stewart, Tim Horton, Carl Brewer, and Frank Mahovlich (in 1960, Dave Keon would graduate from the St. Michael's Majors). But it was players acquired by Imlach in other ways who would eventually make the difference and lead to the Cup. He had an uncanny ability for gathering up other teams' aging or discredited stars, giving up almost nothing in return for them, and extracting from them anywhere up to five or six, or even more, years of valued service. In 1958, for example, he traded the soon-to-be-forgotten Jim

Frank Mahovlich was brought to Toronto from his hometown of Timmins, Ontario at the age of 14 to begin his preparations as the saviour of the Toronto Maple Leafs franchise. Scouted and signed by Bob Davidson, who just managed to sign the talented teenager before Jack Adams arrived in town, Mahovlich joined the St. Michael's Majors of the Ontario Hockey Associations' Jr. A loop. After scoring 52 goals for St. Mike's in 1956-57, Mahovlich was brought up to Toronto for a brief three-game trial at the end of the season, scoring one goal.

Morrison to acquire Allan Stanley, who would give him ten sterling seasons and play on three all-star teams while with the Leafs. He put Red Kelly in a Leaf uniform for the bargain price of Marc Reaume. And it insults reason to consider that he got Johnny Bower, Terry Sawchuk and Bert Olmstead for *no players at all* through the intra-league draft. Among others, he added Eddie Shack, Marcel Pronovost, Andy Bathgate and Al Arbour.

If Imlach had a problem it was that, in his determination to sublimate the individuality of his most talented players to the greater good of the team, he frequently made life miserable for those players. It was this, in addition to his relentless "motivational" hectoring, that drove the free-spirited and talented Carl Brewer into retirement in 1965 and that eventually reduced Frank Mahovlich, the greatest left winger in Leaf history, to an emotional stickpin. On the other hand, it was Imlach who, in 1960, perceived not only the need for a catalyst to convert Mahovlich's enormous potential to some sort of dynamic but exactly what form that catalyst should take. Who but Imlach could have divined that Leonard "Red" Kelly, an aging, sweet-tempered defenceman (the ugliest word in Red's vocabulary was "heck"), could be brought from Detroit, shifted to centre ice after 13 years on the blue line, and so successfully light Frank's fire?

When Frank had joined the Leafs in 1957, he had been nicknamed "The Big M" — "M" for Moses, said King Clancy and, indeed, it was understood that Mahovlich would lead the Leafs into Canaan. And indirectly he did. The facts need little interpretation; the team won four Cups during Frank's years in Toronto and have not won again since he was traded away in 1968. "There were nights," he once said, "when it seemed I could just bull my way through the opposition." At other times he played as if he were protecting a teddy bear, or some delicate missive from the firmament, beneath his jersey.

In Kelly's first full season, 1960-61, Mahovlich fired 48 goals, engaging in a dramatic season-long scoring battle with Montreal's Bernie Geoffrion, who eventually prevailed, becoming the second player in league history to score 50 goals in a season. Six seasons in a row, Frank led the Leafs in goal. But no matter what he did, Imlach would not let him forget that he had never quite reached his potential. During his latter years with the club, Frank twice succumbed to pressure and suffered nervous breakdowns. "There was a delicacy to Frank that Imlach could never leave be," journalist Dick Beddoes once said. "But he could be tough, too. Coaches around the league used to say, 'Just let him drift. Whatever you do, don't wake him up or he'll kill you!'" Mahovlich once beat the daylights out of New York's Bill Gadsby for kneeing him in a centre-ice collision. And in 1961 he incited a brawl against Montreal by accidentally hitting Henri Richard in the mouth with the puck. Before the fight ended, Mahovlich had challenged the entire Montreal bench, an incident Imlach would eventually refer to as Mahovlich's "finest hour."

Imlach's self-expressed intention during those years was to build a team with which he could "beat the Canadiens.... That's

> " Punch (Imlach) was a very, very strict coach. He was a very demanding person. He always expected you to work hard in practice because he felt that what you're gonna do in practice, you're gonna do in a game.
>
> — Johnny Bower

Left to right: Don Simmons, Punch Imlach, Allan Stanley, Ed Litzenberger, Ron Stewart and Dave Keon surround the object of their desires following their emotional six-game victory over Chicago in the 1962 finals. Simmons, who was thrust in the Stanley Cup spotlight when Johnny Bower suffered a leg injury, was exceptional in games five and six as the Leafs won their first title in 11 seasons. Although Simmons would serve as a backup to Bower in 1963 and 1964, he would never play another playoff game. Only weeks after this photo was taken, on June 6, 1962, bush pilot Gary Fields spotted the wreckage of a plane in the deep woods near Cochrane, Ontario. With the discovery, both Bill Barilko and the rumours surrounding his disappearance were laid to rest.

one reason I needed Kelly," he once explained. "He was one guy I could put out against Jean Béliveau and make the big guy fight for every goal he got."

Ironically, when Imlach's first Cup came in 1962, the Leafs did not even have to play the Habs, who had finished first in the league that year but had been knocked off by the defending champs, Chicago, in the semi-finals.

For Leaf fans, the return of the Cup in '62 was like the restoration of some once-great aristocracy, some long-deposed embodiment of their pride and well-being. The downtown victory parade along King Street and up Bay Street to City Hall rivalled the parades that had marked the end of the Second World War. And no one was a bigger hero than Imlach himself, who was perceived as a kind of miracle worker, a man capable of rallying the troops when it mattered.

The Leafs repeated as champs in 1963, defeating the Habs in the semi-finals, and won again in '64, after a desultory season of 33 wins and a third-place finish. The '64 Cup reconfirmed the belief (soon to be abandoned) that Imlach could pretty much win at will.

In the meantime, changes had taken place in Montreal: Jacques

Plante had been dealt to New York, and John Ferguson promoted from the Cleveland Barons. At the end of the 1963-64 season, Frank Selke was urged into retirement and replaced by Sam Pollock, who would proceed with exacting diligence to build the great Canadiens teams of the '70s, as Selke had built for the '50s and '60s. "Sam had a tremendous secret that put him far ahead of the opposition," referee Red Storey once said. "He was very dedicated and worked 18 and 20 hours a day while the other managers worked eight or ten."

"Once you're a winner, you keep improving on perfection," Pollock once said. "You keep making the trades and changes that will strengthen the team, even if they aren't popular at the time. You go about your business. That is where we might have been different from other franchises. Once we started winning, we worked even harder to continue winning. Too many organizations relax at that point."

Pollock didn't have to wait long for his first taste of victory.

The 1964-65 season saw the emergence of a new Habs star, the speedy Yvan Cournoyer. Terry Sawchuk joined Toronto that year and shared Vezina Trophy honours with Johnny Bower. But it was Montreal who won the Cup in the spring, and again the following spring, after a season in which Imlach's Leafs went into noticeable decline.

And the Habs were expected to win again in 1967, after the season's favourites, the first-place Chicago Black Hawks, were eliminated in the semi-finals. But it wasn't to be. The drama and valour of the Leafs' victory that year have been well documented. It was a great year to be a Leafs fan. But, in many ways, it was the last hurrah for the franchise. And it was the last hurrah for the storied rivalry between the Leafs and Canadiens. Traces of the old electricity would remain. But from that point forward, the Leafs

FACING PAGE:
As a general manager, *Punch Imlach wanted players who had "the pride inside." As a coach, he needed players who could withstand his rigorous game-day practices and still have the energy to play sixty minutes of Imlach-instructed hockey. Because George Armstrong, left, and Ron Stewart never questioned his methods, Imlach never had to question their commitment. Players of their ilk tend to avoid the limelight, but after the Leafs polished off the Detroit Red Wings in the 1963 finals, Army and Stew grabbed a fresh glass of bubbly and gave a victory salute that was as much for themselves as it was for the camera.*

would be a diminished force. In the years since, there have been seasons of promise and individual nights of triumph. There have been excellent players and early-round victories in the playoffs. But there have been no Stanley Cups, not even an appearance in the finals.

The Canadiens, on the other hand, have been a model organization — Stanley Cup champions no less than ten times since Canada's centennial year. The great Habs teams of the '70s — a decade in which they won six Stanley Cups — would have given Selke's teams of the '50s a potent, albeit hypothetical, challenge. Like their forebears under Toe Blake, they were effectively coached, now by Scotty Bowman, a Pollock protégé who had been brought back to the Habs from St. Louis after successes there with the expansion Blues. On the ice the Canadiens were a pretty much seamless cohesion of firepower and defence. The players' names alone are redolent of the totality with which they dominated the league during their championship seasons: Guy Lafleur, Larry Robinson, Serge Savard, Guy Lapointe, Yvan Cournoyer, Steve Shutt, Jacques Lemaire, Peter Mahovlich, Ken Dryden. To neutralize other team's shooters, Bowman could deploy Doug Jarvis and Bob Gainey, or Rejean Houle, or Jimmy Roberts, all of whom were among the league's ranking defensive forwards. During the 1976-77 season, the team lost just eight of 80 games, and established a record for team points.

No general manager can match the record of Sam Pollock, who guided the Montreal Canadiens to nine Stanley Cup championships in his 14 seasons in the Habs' front office. Not only was Pollock a shrewd judge of talent, no one was his equal at understanding the machinations of the NHL. He was an expert at recognizing talent before anyone else and he was also adept at acquiring and stockpiling draft choices. From 1969 to 1978, when he retired, the Montreal Canadiens had 26 first-round draft selections. Of the 25 players who wore the bleu, blanc et rouge *on the 1977-78 team – possibly the finest squad of the Pollock era – 20 were homegrown.*

Several of the team's stars — Savard, Cournoyer, Lapointe, Peter and Frank Mahovlich, and particularly goaltender Ken Dryden, an Ivy League graduate and, later, a lawyer — played significant roles in Team Canada's narrow defeat of the Soviets in 1972. But none of them possessed quite the potency of the young Guy Lafleur, who, in 1974, after three frustrating seasons in the league, would take his place as the inheritor of *la ligne*, the

With all the hype that surrounded him, it's not surprising that it took Guy Lafleur some time to adapt to the rigours of playing in the NHL. His first three seasons were marked by inconsistency —he rarely showed glimpses of the "blond demon" he was to become. However, by his fourth season, he began using all his tools— speed, confidence and an overpowering shot—and became the dominant offensive star of the 1970s.

great Canadiens line of succession.

Like Jean Béliveau, Lafleur had had a storied pre-NHL career in Quebec City. As a junior there, he filled the hometown Colisée with worshippers. On the road, he drew capacity crowds in Cornwall, Trois Rivières, Drummondville, Sherbrooke, Verdun. If the Remparts were in town, which is to say if Lafleur was in town, it was all but axiomatic that the local rink would be packed.

When the WHA was formed in 1972, and Lafleur was wooed by the league's new Quebec City franchise, Sam Pollock decided that to let the young prodigy sign with Quebec would so boost the fortunes of the new league and team that the dominance of the Canadiens as the province's premier team could be challenged, even terminated. He countered with an offer that made Lafleur the first Hab with a million-dollar contract.

At the height of his career, Lafleur played with an almost preternatural combination of skills and spirit. There were nights when his physical and motivational edge was practically indefensible to opposition players. However, unlike some of the game's masters — Howe, Hull, Béliveau, Orr — Lafleur was not an "effortless" player. His skating, although mercurial in speed, often seemed

A downtrodden Darryl Sittler looks forlornly at his stick during game five of the 1976 quarter-final series between the Philadelphia Flyers and the Leafs. Goals were definitely hidden inside this piece of lumber; two nights later in Maple Leaf Gardens, Sittler matched Maurice Richard's 1944 benchmark to become only the second player in NHL history to score five goals in one playoff game.

choppy, his moves not entirely efficient; he would swerve, dodge, whirl; he would crash on the brakes at an unexpected moment — always at top energy, and always with an implied glee at what he was doing to frustrate his opponents.

Lafleur led the Canadiens to Stanley Cups four times in succession between 1976 and 1979. Twice during that period the Canadiens met the Leafs in the playoffs, the first time in a 1978 semi-final, after the Leafs had defeated the emergent New York Islanders. The Leafs of that period were competitive up to a point. They had two of the finest forwards in the league, in Darryl Sittler and Lanny MacDonald; they had a tough guy in Tiger Williams, and a pair of all-star defencemen, Ian Turnbull and Borje Salming. While Sittler, MacDonald, Williams and Turnbull had come up through the Canadian junior leagues, Salming was an anomaly at the time, a European player not only of great skill but of superior

"I flew over there and took in the hockey game the next day and Borje Salming just stood out ... I phoned Jim Gregory, who was in Toronto, and said 'Is there anybody on the negotiation list that's not very good? Get rid of him.' He says 'We got one spot open.' I said, 'That's good. Put Borje Salming in that spot."

— Bob Davidson

Borje Salming wasn't the first Swede defenseman to play in the NHL (that honour goes to Thommie Bergman), but he was the best. There has been some speculation that Salming would never have become a Maple Leaf if team owner Harold Ballard hadn't been in jail when scout Bob Davidson signed him after spotting him at the 1973 World Championships. A six-time All-Star, Salming went on to play 16 seasons with the Leafs, and is the team's all-time leader with 620 career assists.

"I used to laugh (when) people talked about the 'mystique' of the Canadiens. There's no mystique to the Canadiens. The mystique of the Canadiens is that you've got twenty guys going out there and working to their maximum capabilities."

— Steve Shutt

Sam Pollock made the trade that gave him the fourth-overall pick in the 1972 Amateur Draft way back in 1968, and he used the selection to steal Toronto-native Steve Shutt from under the nose of the Maple Leafs. A smooth-skating left winger with a howitzer for a shot, Shutt scored at least 30 goals in nine consecutive seasons for the Canadiens.

toughness and strength. Far from wilting or turning the other cheek when his courage was tested by rugged NHL checkers, Salming took his lumps and gave them back. During a couple of playoff series against the Philadelphia Flyers in the mid-'70s, the Swedish defenceman traded elbows and hostilities with the meanest of NHL pros and never so much as flinched. His stylish play earned him all-star recognition six times between 1975 and 1980. Indeed, he was the first European to be named an all-star and, until 1984, when Jari Kurri was selected, the only European to be so honoured.

But even with Salming and Sittler, the Leafs' talent at the time was never quite strong or cohesive enough to derail the Habs. For every star in the Toronto line-up, there were two in Montreal, and the Habs made short work of the Leafs in both of their playoff encounters during the late 1970s.

The divergence in the two clubs' paths at this point can be reduced to a word: management.

It might well be said that the Leafs' woes began in 1961 when, under pressure from his son Stafford, Conn Smythe gave up control of the Gardens to Stafford, John Bassett and Harold Ballard. Throughout the early and mid-'60s, the spirit of the senior Smythe prevailed. But it wasn't long before the imperative to win had given way to a more venal desire for pure profit.

The owners' miserly attitudes did not hurt the hockey operation directly until 1968, when as a cost-saving measure Ballard and Smythe sold the club's two minor-league pro teams, the Victoria Maple Leafs and the Rochester Americans. The club had also lost players in the previous year's expansion draft, with the result that over the next few years they sank gradually in the standings, finishing last in their division in 1969-70 and missing the playoffs for the second time in three years. By this time, Imlach had been fired.

The Canadiens kept their farm clubs, trading seasoned players to needy expansion clubs for draft picks. While the Habs were gathering up draft picks that would bring them such players as Guy Lafleur, Larry Robinson, Steve Shutt and Bob Gainey, the Leafs had no extra players to trade — it was all they could do to ice a team that hovered around the .500 mark.

In addition, the Leafs reduced their scouting staff, which made for fewer prospects, particularly from the talented overseas market and the burgeoning pool of NHL-calibre players coming from U.S. colleges.

By 1972, the debacle at Maple Leaf Gardens had reached extreme proportions. The eminently reasonable John Bassett had been bought out by his partners, Stafford Smythe was dead, and Harold Ballard, a miserly eccentric, had gained control of the building and hockey club.

What's more, the founding of the WHA had thrown a king-sized wrench into the already fragile workings of the club. Competition between leagues for players forced salaries out of control and resulted in the immediate loss of key Leaf players such as Rick Ley, Jim Harrison and Bernie Parent. Between 1972 and 1979, when four surviving WHA franchises joined the NHL, the Leafs lost 18 players in all, including Norm Ullman, Blaine Stoughton and captain Dave Keon.

The Canadiens, too, lost players to the new league, current general manager Rejean Houle, Marc Tardif and J.C. Tremblay among them. But the Habs had players with which to replace their losses. The Leafs did not.

Ballard's ascendancy introduced the darkest period in Maple Leaf history, an 18-year farce that began with his being sent to prison for income-tax evasion (he served nearly a year; and would have had Stafford Smythe as a prison mate had the latter not died) and ended with his death in 1990.

Between those notable events, the organization sank into disgrace. Ballard hired cronies and toadies to fill management positions, rather than competent hockey people, and players and employees were shabbily treated. The building deteriorated to the point where, for several years, large plastic sheets had to be suspended from the rafters to catch the drips of water that came through the roof.

Ballard's parsimonious habits and mammoth ego became a manifest joke. Building superintendent Wayne Gilespie recalls that one day Ballard inquired as to how many cucumbers would fit in the 30,000-gallon brine tank — a holding vessel for salt water and toxic chemicals that are pumped out at sub-zero temperatures through refrigeration pipes beneath the ice. "He said he wanted to make dill pickles to sell at games," says Gilespie. "He'd dream up these schemes — anything to make a buck — then he'd forget about them."

On another occasion, Ballard got Gardens employees to help him make imprints of his hands and feet in the concrete beneath centre ice. The imprints, complete with a brass-lettered inscrip-

Pal Hal was here. *Harold Ballard's hand and footprints adorn the concrete beneath the centre-ice faceoff spot in Maple Leaf Gardens.*

tion, were originally filled with epoxy, which created inconsistencies in the quality of the ice above them. The epoxy was removed and the imprints filled with concrete at the first opportunity following Ballard's death.

It is a testimony to the traditions of the institution — as well as to hope and nostalgia — that despite the Maple Leafs' poor level of play and the ongoing ownership absurdities of the 1970s and '80s that the fans kept filling the seats and the money kept rolling in.

In the years following Ballard's death, control fell first to Donald Giffin and then, not without controversy, to current majority owner Steve Stavro, both of whom made moves that they believed would stabilize the franchise. Giffin hired Cliff Fletcher as general manager and president, hoping that Fletcher would bring to Toronto some of the success he had enjoyed with the Calgary Flames. Fletcher improved the team's fortunes by hiring coach Pat Burns from the Canadiens, and by trading for players such as Doug Gilmour and Mats Sundin, who now play alongside original Leaf draft picks Wendel Clark and goaltender Felix Potvin. In 1993 and '94, the team made it as far as the league semi-finals, igniting the hopes of Torontonians and the Leaf fans who remain across the country.

But over the past couple of years an old Leaf syndrome has reappeared, the making of questionable trades, and the team now finds itself with an aging roster and few prospects with which to rebuild.

Meanwhile, the Habs of the '80s and '90s, have been a pared-down success story, occasionally evoking echoes of the great teams of the past. In 1978, Irving Grundman took over from Sam Pollock as managing director, but the move eventually proved unsatisfactory. Playoff upsets at the hands of the Minnesota North Stars, Edmonton Oilers and Buffalo Sabres combined with disappointing results from a succession of first-round draft choices brought the Grundman era to an end.

In April of 1983, the organization's top hockey job was given to the Habs' Hall-of-Fame defenceman Serge Savard. In 1986, Savard won his first Stanley Cup, with a team that featured the brilliant goaltending of rookie Patrick Roy and the nettlesome creativity of another rookie, Claude Lemieux (both players, coincidentally, eventually ended up with the Colorado Avalanche and played decisive roles in that club's Cup triumph of 1996). The winning

Claude Lemieux, one of a batch of talented Montreal rookies *who rose above their inexperience during the 1986 playoffs, gives the traditional Stanley Cup salute after the Canadiens won the league championship in five games over Calgary. Lemieux, whose dramatic overtime goal in game seven of the quarter-final series against Hartford allowed Montreal to advance, played only 10 games during the regular season. However, in the playoffs his tenacious checking and timely scoring kept him in the lineup and he responded with 16 points in 20 play-off games to lead all rookie marksmen.*

goal in 1986 was scored by Bobby Smith, who was brought by Savard from Minnesota and whose playing style was often compared to that of Jean Béliveau.

Savard's dealing came up trumps again in 1993. By that time, he had hired coach Jacques Demers and reinforced the team's core — Patrick Roy, Guy Carbonneau and Eric Desjardins, among others — with youngsters such as Stephan Lebeau and Benoit Brunet, obtained in the draft, and with a brace of veterans from other teams, including Kirk Muller, Brian Bellows, Denis Savard and Vincent Damphousse. The team had played well enough to finish third in the Adams Division during the season, but in the playoffs enjoyed astounding good fortune. Eleven times during the playoffs they went into overtime, and ten times in a row they came out victors. It was a year in which the Maple Leafs very nearly defeated the Los Angeles Kings in the semi-finals — a near "victory" that, had it occurred, would, as in days past, have put the Leafs

Toronto's first selection in the 1986 Entry Draft, Vincent Damphousse spent five productive seasons with the Leafs. In 1989-90, he established a team record for points by a left-winger with 94. Traded to Edmonton in the deal that brought Grant Fuhr and Glenn Anderson to the Leafs, Damphousse found his way to the Canadiens in 1992. He posted a 97-point season in 1992-93, joining Frank Mahovlich as the only players to lead both the Leafs and the Canadiens in regular-season scoring.

Two popular journeymen players with the Canadiens' dynasty teams of the 1970s were hired as the general manager and coach of the club in 1995 despite having no previous front office experience. Rejean Houle, far left, was named g.m. while Mario Tremblay became the Habs' 22nd head coach.

> " *The people who were here before us succeeded on the ice and off. We feel the pressure that we have to succeed, too.* "
> — Rejean Houle

and Habs into contention for the Cup. And for a few giddy days, fans of both teams savoured the possibility. But fate and Wayne Gretzky put an end to the Leafs that year — and to the prospect of a classic final series matchup in the Cup's centennial year.

Since then, the Habs have undergone significant changes. Serge Savard was fired and replaced by his one-time teammate Rejean Houle early in the 1995-96 season, and coach Jacques Demers has been replaced behind the bench by former player Mario Tremblay. While this young club was anything but dominant during its first season under Tremblay and Houle, it was competitive and entertaining, showing positive signs for the future. The Leafs, on the other hand, have a veteran core and have squandered rookies and draft picks. Club president Cliff Fletcher — a master roster builder — has a lengthy and difficult reconstruction job ahead.

With that in mind, the future does not bode well for the old rivalry. What's more, the teams are now in different conferences and meet just twice a season. And yet for those who remember what was — Richard and Kennedy; Plante and Bower; Ferguson and Shack; Béliveau, Mahovlich and Keon — there will always be an added measure of excitement on those rare occasions when the teams take to the ice. There will also be a hope, however faint, that the legendary tensions of the past will recreate themselves on the ice as they do time and again as flashpoints of memory and imagination.

FOREVER
RIVALS
THE GOALTENDERS

Although all records are made to be broken, *it is safe to assume that no goaltender will ever match Montreal Canadiens' netminder George Hainsworth's incredible 22 shutouts in 44 games during the 1928-29 season. Interestingly, the Canadiens won only 22 games that season, recording seven 0-0 ties.*

Bill Durnan and Turk Broda *may have been adversaries on the ice, but they had a great respect for each other when the battle was over, as this photo indicates. Their post-NHL careers took similar roads. Both men went into coaching, Durnan at the senior level, Broda in junior, but neither man was given the opportunity to coach in the NHL. Ironically, they died within days of each other in the fall of 1972.*

Gerry McNeil had the unenviable task of replacing Bill Durnan in the Montreal crease, but he proved that he was equal to the task in the 1952-53 season. McNeil, who led the league with 10 shutouts during the regular campaign, recorded an NHL-best 1.98 GAA during the playoffs.

In his first full NHL of 1950-51, Al Rollins compiled an impressive 27-5-8 record with an NHL-leading goals-against average of 1.77. But he didn't take rookie of the year honours. Rollins lost the Calder Trophy race to Terry Sawchuk, but he did capture a worthy consolation prize, winning the Vezina Trophy.

Ed Chadwick was a relative unknown when he was summoned from the WHL's Winnipeg Warriors during the 1955-56 season. Five games later, the Leafs were on the phone taking trade requests for incumbent Harry Lumley after Chadwick hand-cuffed the opposition by recording two shutouts and a 0.60 GAA in his five-game trial. By the time the 1956-57 season opened, Lumley was in Chicago and Chadwick was the Leafs' #1 goaltender. A "cage cop" in the truest sense of the phrase, Chadwick was employed as a policeman in his home town of Keswick, Ontario during the off-season.

No goaltender revolutionized the way the position was played more than Jacques Plante, arguably the greatest netminder in the history of the game.

Plante was the first goaltender to leave the confines of the crease to actively participate in the game. He would stop the puck behind the net for his defensemen, pass the puck up ice to his teammates, dive out of the crease to smother loose pucks and clear the puck around the boards away from oncoming forwards.

Although Plante often wore a face mask in practice, *coach Toe Blake wouldn't allow him to use facial protection in a game. This gave Plante time to "field test" his design for the mask, and by the time he finally had the opportunity to wear it in regular action, he had already built and improved upon a pair of prototypes.*

"

Jacques (Plante) was the best goalie I've ever seen ... We'd always say that in an important game you couldn't get an aspirin by him. The bigger the game, the better he played. He didn't get credit at the start because the team in front of him was pretty good, but Jacques was the key man and the best goaltender I've ever seen. And that was in the era of Terry Sawchuk, who was also very good."

— Tom Johnson

A smiling Terry Sawchuk shares a chuckle with goaltending partner Johnny Bower during the 1967 play-offs. Sawchuk rarely smiled. Before, after and especially during games, he was totally immersed in his own private purgatory. Sawchuk's remarkable career was winding down when he was drafted by Toronto in June 1964, but he managed to turn in one of his greatest performances in the 1967 playoffs.

"
Terry Sawchuk was a loner ... After a game, he'd go his own way. He didn't mix too much with the other players but you can't hold that against him. He was still a great competitor and a great goaltender. His record speaks for itself."
— Johnny Bower

In his first season in Toronto, Terry Sawchuk, left, combined with Johnny Bower to create the NHL's top goaltending tandem. The pair shared the Vezina Trophy in the 1964-65 season, allowing only 173 goals in 70 games.

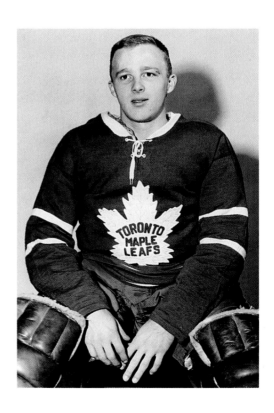

The Toronto Maple Leaf organization was rich in talent during the early 1960s, especially in goal. Gerry Cheevers, who played only two games with the Leafs before being acquired by Boston, was just one horse in a stable that also included Cesare Maniago, Bruce Gamble, Gil Mayer, Gerry McNamara, Al Smith and Gary Smith.

One of the first moves Sam Pollock made as general manager of the Montreal Canadiens was to acquire the rights to a 17-year-old goaltender named Ken Dryden from Boston in June 1964. By the time Dryden made his first appearance in the NHL in March 1971, he was a graduate of Cornell University and had completed a brief tour of duty with Canada's National Team. Dryden's book about his playing days in Montreal, simply titled **The Game,** remains the best testimonial on the sport and the personalities that play it.

Mike Palmateer's acrobatic goaltending *and energetic style made him a fan favorite at Maple Leaf Gardens throughout his six season stay with Toronto. Palmateer's first career shutout was a 1-0 win at the expense of the Canadiens on November 17, 1976. A pair of wonky knees brought his career to a premature end, but Leaf enthusiasts still rave about the "Popcorn Kid."*

His time in the spotlight *was brief, but for one month during the 1984 playoffs no goaltender was better than Steve Penney. Penney appeared in only four games for the Habs during the regular season, but he started all of the Canadiens 15 postseason games. The Habs swept the Bruins in three straight and won the second installment of the "Battle of Quebec" by beating the Nordiques in six games before losing to the defending Stanley Cup-champion New York Islanders. Penney led all playoff goaltenders with three shutouts and a 2.20 GAA.*

Although Cliff Fletcher *was criticized for acquiring Grant Fuhr in September 1991, he knew he was gaining an important trump card for use in the future. Fuhr was invaluable in helping Felix Potvin mature, and when Potvin proved he was ready to handle the #1 goaltending job, Fletcher was able to dispatch Fuhr to Buffalo in exchange for super-sniper Dave Andreychuk.*

Patrick Roy keeps his eye on the prize and in Montreal that was usually post-season silverware. The road to Stanley Cup success in Montreal begins and ends in goal, where the line of ascension stretched from Georges Vezina to Patrick Roy and, now, Jocelyn Thibault. An unheralded rookie when he took over the top goaltending chores during the 1985-86 season, Roy didn't begin to shine until the playoffs, when he was close to unbeatable in leading the Canadiens to a surprising Stanley Cup victory.

Felix Potvin became the first Maple Leaf rookie since Al Rollins to lead the league in goals-against-average when he topped all NHL goalies with a 2.50 GAA in 1992-93. He notched his first NHL shutout against Montreal, blanking the Habs 4-0 on January 23, 1993.

In a tumultuous start to the 1995-96 season, star goaltender Patrick Roy demanded to be traded only weeks after the Canadiens had changed their general manager and coach. Roy and team captain Mike Keane were dispatched to Colorado for goalie Jocelyn Thibault and forwards Martin Rucinsky and Andrei Kovalenko. Thibault, seen here sprawling to stop Mike Gartner's scoring attempt, was the key to the deal. A young, Quebec-born goalie whose style is not unlike that of Roy's, Thibault went on to win 23 games in 1995-96, one more than Roy.

FOREVER
RIVALS
1900 • 1939

No one did more to help establish the Toronto Maple Leafs as "Canada's Team" than radio play-by-play pioneer Foster Hewitt. With his nasal tone, constant banter and limitless enthusiasm, Hewitt's weekly Leaf broadcasts would attract millions of listeners from St. John's to Victoria. In fact, Hewitt became as popular as the team itself, and he used that notoriety to build a powerful media empire in southern Ontario.

> "
> *Everybody from the West listened to Foster Hewitt. When I came down [to Montreal], that was one of my biggest thrills; to make the team, play in Maple Leaf Gardens and have Foster Hewitt broadcasting and your friends and parents hearing about you out west."*
>
> -- *Kenny Reardon*

*A **large bandage** above the left eye of Newsy Lalonde, left, doesn't appear to dampen his enthusiasm for this team picture in 1911-12. Goaltender Georges Vezina is the other Canadien in this photo. "CAC" on these striped red-white-and-blue sweaters stands for Club Athlétique Canadien."*

"Bad" Joe Hall obtained his nasty nickname after being expelled from the Manitoba Senior League for rough play in 1905. A continual thorn in the side of any forward who skated near him, Hall also earned a well-deserved reputation as one of the game's outstanding defenders. During the 1919 Stanley Cup finals in Seattle, Hall fell victim to the influenza epidemic that eventually claimed the life of Canadiens team owner George Kendall. Hall was hospitalized, along with several of his teammates, causing the championship series to be cancelled. He died in a Seattle hospital on April 5, 1919.

As he checked his shopping list prior to the opening of Maple Leafs Gardens in 1931, Conn Smythe realized he needed an experienced playoff performer. When the Ottawa Senators asked for a leave of absence from the NHL for the 1931-32 season, Smythe stepped in a grabbed Frank Finnigan off the Ottawa roster. Finnigan, an eight-year veteran who played a reliable two-way game, gave the Leafs a solid second-line winger and an expert penalty-killer. After playing a key role in the Leafs' 1932 Stanley Cup victory, Finnigan was returned to Ottawa. When that franchise finally folded after one year in St. Louis, Finnigan rejoined the Leafs and finished his career in Toronto.

Joe Malone's illusive skating style *and deceptive dekes earned him the nickname "Phantom Joe" during his Hall-of-Fame career. In his first season wearing the Canadiens' uniform, he led the newly-formed National Hockey League in scoring with 44 goals in only 20 games. Although he spent only 57 games with Montreal, he served as a model for the classy, flying Frenchmen that followed him.*

Conn Smythe continued *to
manage and coach the Leafs and
although Alex Romeril was
often behind the bench, it was
Smythe who pulled the strings.
Art Duncan was officially
named as coach in 1930, but
when the club went winless in
the first five games of the 1931-
32 campaign, Smythe went
shopping. With a new arena and
a underachieving hockey team,
Smythe needed fresh blood and
stern discipline. He found both
in Dick Irvin, who had been cut
loose in Chicago despite leading
the Black Hawks to the 1931
Cup finals. Irvin was a no-non-
sense competitor whose playing
career was cut short because of a
serious head injury. He pushed
all the right buttons and guided
the Leafs to a Stanley Cup
championship in 1932.*

This store window display celebrates the Canadiens' second consecutive Stanley Cup championship in 1931. The Habs were an injured lot going into game one of the finals versus Chicago. Battleship Leduc, Armand Mondou, Pit Lepine and Howie Morenz were all nursing various ailments. The Canadiens won game one 2-1 and then lost two overtime contests before coming back to win the last two games of the series. The final goal of game five was scored by Morenz, his only goal of the playoffs. During Montreal's semi-final series with Boston, Bruins coach Art Ross removed goaltender Tiny Thompson late in game two in an unsuccessful attempt to get the tying goal. This was the first time that a goalie had been pulled in favour of a sixth attacker in Stanley Cup play.

" Personally, I've always felt that a great hockey player is like a great artist, and a great artist has a tendency to be an individual. But if you put those great artists together, I think that's what makes a championship."

— Jean Béliveau

Irvine "Ace" Bailey, the Toronto Maple Leafs' first superstar, was an energetic winger with a delicate touch around the net. A unselfish player, Bailey was prepared to assume any role to help the team win. It was that dedication that eventually cost him his career. He was filling in along the blueline for a rushing King Clancy when he was upended by Boston's Eddie Shore and suffered a fractured skull. Although his playing days were over, Bailey stayed involved in the game, coaching at the junior, senior and collegiate levels and working as an off-ice official at Maple Leaf Gardens.

When it became clear that Ace Bailey's head injuries would end his career, *league officials gathered to discuss ways of supporting Bailey and his family. No player pension plan existed at the time, so the NHL decided to stage an exhibition game between the Maple Leafs and a team of All-Stars (pictured above), with the proceeds going to Bailey and his family. On February 14, 1934, in front of a packed house at Maple Leaf Gardens, the Leafs—dubbed the "Aces" for this game—delivered a special Valentine's Day present to their recovering teammate by downing the All-Stars 7-3 and raising $23,000 for the Bailey household.*

The trinity that ruled the Leafs blue-line from 1931 to 1936: (from left to right) Reginald "Red" Horner, Frank "King" Clancy and Clarence "Hap" Day. Horner supplied muscle and mayhem, Clancy delivered energy and enthusiasm and Day provided consistency and commitment.

Another outstanding prospect from western Canada who was signed by superscout Squib Walker, Frank "Buzz" Boll played six years with the Leafs. Boll was content to stay out of the headlines and play his consistent well-rounded game. However, in the the 1936 playoffs with both Charlie Conacher and Busher Jackson nursing nagging injuries, Boll stepped into the spotlight. He led all playoff scorers with seven goals and ten points and helped propel the Leafs into the championship finals against Detroit. These would prove to be the only post-season points of his 11-year career.

RIDERS OF THE OPEN PLAINS

The Alexandra Studios in Toronto, under the watchful guidance of Lou and Nat Turofsky, were the official photographers of the Toronto Maple Leafs for almost 40 years. In addition to providing a visual history of the franchise and its players, the Turofsky brothers also created unique photo-collages to advertise upcoming games and help keep the seats full at Maple Leaf Gardens. "Riders of the open plains" and "They're off! Watch their smoke" are just two examples of their art and craft. In fact, keeping the seats "full" was one of their mandates. Conn Smythe told the Turofsky's that every time one of their action photos showed an empty seat, they owed him a new fedora.

FOREVER
RIVALS
1940 • 1959

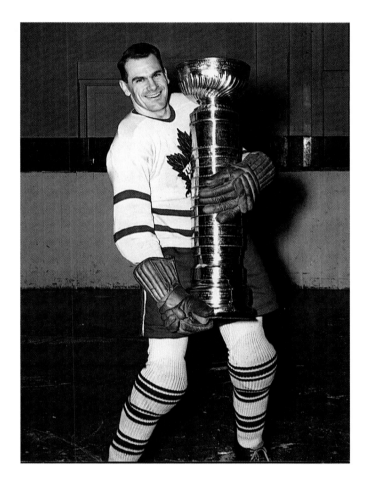

Syl Apps cradles the "cigar-shaped" Stanley Cup after the Leafs
astonishing come-from-behind victory in the 1942 Finals. After dropping
the first three games to Detroit, coach Hap Day made a number of tactical
changes and roster amendments. He benched some key veterans (Gordie
Drillon and Bucko McDonald) and added some young players (Don Metz
and Gaye Stewart) to increase his team speed. Day was then able to neutralize the Wings "dump-and-chase" attack by using his defensemen to
cut off the skating lanes and his fastest forwards to reach any shoot-in
before the Detroit attackers. Toronto went on to win the next four games
to become the only team in professional sports history to win a best-of-
seven championship round after losing the first three matches.

When the deal was announced on February 13, 1936, it didn't rate much more than a quick mention in the local newspapers. But it was a turning point in the history of the Canadiens franchise. The Montreal Canadiens sent goaltender Lorne Chabot, who hadn't been able to crack the lineup, to the Montreal Maroons for a trio of prospects: Ken Grivel, Bill Miller and Hec Blake. Grivel never made the grade and Miller only wore the Habs colours for 17 games, but Blake became "Toe" and went on to win ten Stanley Cup titles as a player and coach.

One of the greatest upsets in NHL history occurred during the 1945 playoffs. The Toronto Maple Leafs, who finished 28 points behind the defending champion Montreal Canadiens, shocked the hockey establishment by dropping the Habs in a six game semi-final, thanks to an outstanding game plan designed by Hap Day and carried out to perfection by his players. Day realized they couldn't stop Montreal's explosive "Punch Line" of Lach, Richard and Blake, but he could contain them with tight coverage. Bob Davidson covered Rocket Richard like a blanket and Nick Metz was in Elmer Lach's back pocket through the entire series. The Leafs side-stepped the Habs and outlasted Detroit to win their third Stanley Cup title.

An excited group of Maple Leaf players jump over the boards to celebrate Syl Apps' overtime goal that gave Toronto a 2-1 win over Montreal in game four of the 1947 Stanley Cup finals. The gentleman with the fedora and moustache in the lower left part of the photo is Camil DesRoches, who was the head of the Canadiens publicity department. He was making his way to the lobby to phone the train station with a request that the Habs express back to Montreal be delayed when Apps potted the game-winner.

Howie Meeker, seen here with Coach Day, *sealed his bid for Calder Trophy honours on January 8, 1947, when he became the first rookie in NHL history to score five goals in a single game. The mere fact that Meeker was playing hockey was worthy of an award. While serving in the Canadian army in World War II, a grenade exploded at his feet, lacerating his legs. After a lengthy recovery period, Meeker returned to Canada and to hockey, suiting up with the Stratford Seniors for the 1945-46 season. Meeker made the Leafs' club in training camp in 1946 and went on to play eight seasons with the team.*

Nick Metz, left, Hap Day and Wally Stanowski put a hug on the mug after the Leafs defeated the Detroit Red Wings 7-2 to sweep the 1948 finals in straight games. Moments later, Metz took off his uniform for the last time, putting an end to his often underrated 12-year career. Never a proficient scorer, Metz was content to play an aggressive forechecking style, skills he learned under the tutelage of Father Athol Murray at Notre Dame College in Wilcox, Saskatchewan. He is still regarded as one of the greatest defensive forwards to ever play the game.

Two Canadiens – Elmer Lach and Maurice Richard – and one Maple Leaf – Turk Broda – were named to the NHL's First All-Star Team in 1947-48 (left to right: coach Tommy Ivan, "Black Jack" Stewart, Lach, Bill Quackenbush, Broda, NHL president Clarence Campbell, Richard and "Terrible" Ted Lindsay). These future Hall of Famers pose for the camera prior to the start of the second annual NHL All-Star Game at Maple Leaf Gardens.

Before the start of the 1947-48 season, Leaf captain Syl Apps told Conn Smythe he was going to play until he scored 200 career goals, and then he was going to retire. With the impending loss of Apps on the timetable, Smythe immediately began making plans to acquire another dominant center. The best in the business—shown here—was the "Dipsy-Doodling-Dandy-from-Delisle," Max Bentley of the Chicago Black Hawks. Six games into the 1947-48 campaign, Smythe sent five players—including the entire "Boxcar Line" of Bodnar, Stewart and Poile—to Chicago to obtain the classy playmaker.

The changing of the guard in Toronto
was complete when captain Ted Kennedy
accepted the Stanley Cup from Clarence
Campbell after the Leafs clipped the Detroit
Red Wings in the 1949 Stanley Cup finals.
It was a sweet victory for both Kennedy
and the Leafs. With Nick Metz and Syl
Apps both retired, Kennedy was thrust
into the spotlight as the team's offensive
and inspirational leader. When the Leafs
struggled just to make the playoffs, many
scribes questioned Kennedy's leadership.
But Teeder roused the troops and once the
Leafs reached the post-season spotlight,
they stole the show. The club dropped only
one game in the playoffs (an overtime loss
to Boston in the semi-finals) as they set an
NHL record with their third consecutive
Stanley Cup triumph.

Whoever penned the phrase "all things must pass" never met Cal Gardner or Ken Reardon. Both men still carry a grudge over a pair of fouls that occurred almost 50 years ago. The feud started on the final night of the 1947-48 season when Reardon ran face first into Gardner's stick and lost a pair of his favourite teeth. In their first meeting the following season, both men engaged in a wild stick-swing duel that left both men weak in the wallet but otherwise unharmed. Reardon seemingly evened the score later that season when a well-placed shoulder broke both sides of Gardner's jaw. But Reardon wanted blood, not broken bones. Before the start of the 1949-50 season, Reardon told a sportswriter that he was going to "cut Gardner for at least 14 stitches even if it takes the rest of my NHL career." With that, President Clarence Campbell had heard enough. He ordered Reardon to post a $1,000 bond, insuring that he would not purposely injure Gardner. Reardon retired after the 1950 season but both men have continued to trade body blows, in print at least, ever since.

> " There was no swearing, no nothing. [Hap Day] just coached behind the bench. 'You're next. Then you. Do what you have to do,' and I think it worked out fine."
>
> — Cal Gardner

In 1950, Hap Day moved upstairs to become assistant general manager. His replacement was Joe Primeau, left, who already had a pair of Memorial Cup titles and an Allan Cup championship on his resume. Primeau would quickly add a Stanley Cup banner to his trophy room, thanks to his sound defensive strategy and the efforts of, left to right, Ted Kennedy, Jim Thompson, Harry Watson, Sid Smith, Tod Sloan and Gus Mortson.

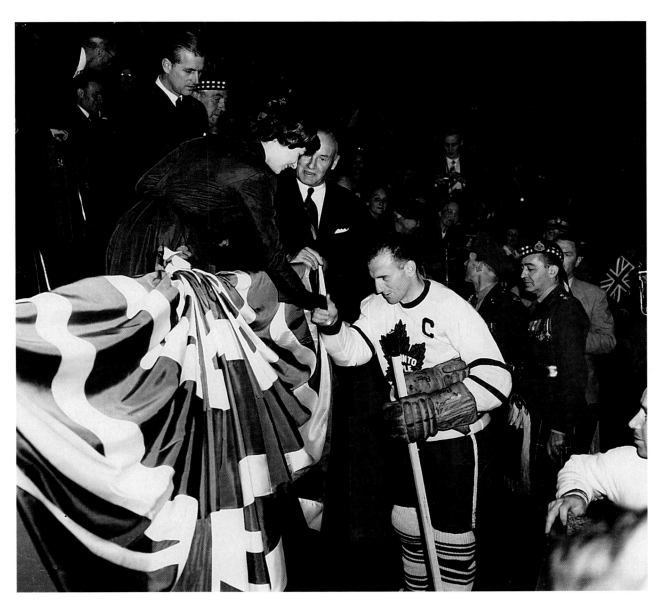

As captain of the Toronto Maple Leafs, *Ted Kennedy was presented to HRH Princess Elizabeth and her husband Philip, the Duke of Edinburgh, during the couple's tour of Canada in October, 1951. The Princess and Duke were treated to a special 15-minute exhibition game between the Maple Leafs and Chicago that was held prior to their scheduled match on October 21, 1951. Although the royal party was behind schedule, the Princess insisted they stay for the entire period before departing.*

As Elmer Lach looks on, *Canadiens coach Dick Irvin peels off bills for Norm Dussault after the Montreal centre scored the winning goal in a 2-1 victory over the Toronto Maple Leafs on March 22, 1950. When Conn Smythe heard rumours that Irvin had offered a $100 reward to any player who could score the winning goal against the Leafs, he demanded that Irvin be fined $2000 under the NHL bylaw that punishes any coach for "agreeing to pay a bonus to a player as a special inducement to a player to win a game." However, league president Clarence Campbell side-stepped the issue by insisting that the money was an award, not a bonus.*

Both Sid Smith, left, and Fleming Mackell played *pivotal roles in Toronto's victory over Boston in the 1951 semi-finals. Mackell collected five points in the six-game series, while Smith chipped in with a pair of goals and two assists. The Bruins were so impressed by Mackell's efforts they traded promising defenseman Jim Morrison to the Leafs to acquire him. Although Mackell helped carry Boston to the finals three times in the 1950s, his only Cup ring came with the Leafs in 1951.*

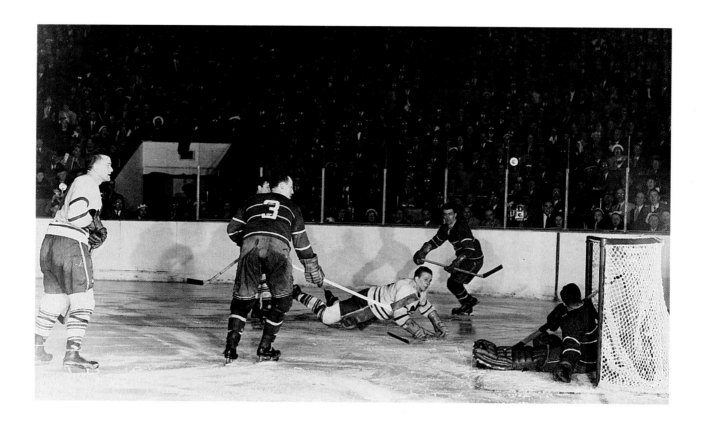

Two contrasting views of the most celebrated goal in the history of Maple Leaf Gardens—Bill Barilko's Stanley Cup-winning goal in overtime during the 1951 finals. The goal itself was the result of a broken play. Howie Meeker had thrown the puck out in front of the net just as he was being slammed into the end boards by Tom Johnson. Harry Watson, who was cruising through the slot, collected Meeker's feed and fired the puck toward Gerry McNeil in the Habs' goal. However, the puck deflected off Montreal defenseman Butch Bouchard's skate and spun toward the face-off circle. With everyone's attention focused on the net, Barilko was able to sneak in from the blueline and, with one diving/sweeping motion, backhand the puck toward the Canadiens' net. McNeil, who had dropped to the ice when Watson had shot, was hopelessly out of position and could only reach in vain as the puck soared over his blocker and into history.

By the end of the 1955 season, *Dick Irvin was in failing health and unable to find the energy needed to control Rocket Richard, his volatile star. Midway through the 1954-55 season, Chicago Black Hawk owner Jim Norris had approached the Canadiens for permission to negotiate with Irvin when the season ended. At the time Frank Selke told Norris the decision would be left up to Irvin, but that was before the Rocket's suspension, the riot and the seven-game loss to Detroit. After the final bell, Selke told Irvin that he was through as coach, but he could stay in the organization. Irvin decided to go back to Chicago, where his coaching career began. He passed away less than two years later. At right, Richard appeals for calm after the rioting that followed his suspension in March of 1955.*

Early in his career, more than a few players challenged Jean Béliveau to prove he belonged in the league. And to his credit, Béliveau never backed down from any adversary. During the 1955-56 season, the year in which he won his only scoring title and captured his first Hart Trophy as league MVP, he accumulated 143 minutes in penalties, a club record to that time.

The Montreal Canadiens' dedication to team defense was an integral ingredient in the franchise's five-year dynasty from 1956 to 1960. That smothering defense, seen in evidence here as Claude Provost (14), Doug Harvey (2) and Bob Turner (11) surround Billy Harris, allowed the Canadiens to lead the NHL in goals-against in five consecutive seasons. Turner was a classic stay-at-home defenseman whose conservative style perfectly complemented Doug Harvey's offensive flair.

The 1955-56 season was difficult for Butch Bouchard. Injuries and age finally caught up with the burly defenseman and he spent the majority of the campaign watching from the sidelines as rookie rearguards Jean-Guy Talbot and Bob Turner took his place along the blueline. In the playoffs, he dressed for almost every game but his contribution was limited to providing moral support. His skates never touched the ice. In the final minute of the final game of the finals, with the Stanley Cup safely in the Habs' grasp, coach Toe Blake finally gave Bouchard the nod and he jumped over the boards for the final face-off of his career. Moments later, he returned to the ice to accept the Stanley Cup for the last time as captain of the Montreal Canadiens.

LA REVUE SPORTIVE du *Forum* SPORTS MAGAZINE

25¢

Tom Johnson

SAISON 1959-60 SEASON — L'ORGANE OFFICIEL des CANADIENS et and ROYALS OFFICIAL PUBLICATION

LA 51ème SAISON DES CANADIENS — LA 34ème DU ROYAL
LES CANADIENS' 51st SEASON — ROYALS' 34th SEASON

A game program from the Montreal Forum featuring Baldur, Manitoba, native Tom Johnson. For much of his career, Johnson played in the shadow of teammate Doug Harvey, but he stepped into the limelight during the 1958-59 campaign, capturing the Norris Trophy and a First Team All-Star berth. The Forum was also home to the Canadiens' top farm club, the Montreal Royals, that began play in 1926. The club won the Allan Cup in 1947, the Quebec League crown in 1959 and the Eastern Pro League title in 1960 before folding in 1961. Many of the Habs' top stars, including Plante, Harvey, Johnson, Moore, Durnan and St. Laurent, graduated to the Canadiens from the Royals.

"(Montreal) is a great city to play in ... but if things were going bad, you didn't want to walk down Ste. Catherine Street because people would be bugging you a little. You'd walk down the back alleys or you'd stay home. It was expected of you to win. You weren't expected to do anything else. We expected every year to go out and win the league and win the Stanley Cup."

— Tom Johnson

Jean Béliveau, left, and Bert Olmstead take a breather before waging another on-ice war with the Maple Leafs. Olmstead later joined Toronto and played a major role in helping the Maple Leafs win the Stanley Cup title in 1961-62. However, after the victory, the Leafs placed Olmstead on waivers, and he was claimed by the New York Rangers for the $20,000 waiver price. When Olmstead refused to report to the Rangers, the club suspended him. Olmstead was forbidden to play or coach at any level as long as the ban was in place. He even tried to be reinstated as an amateur so he could join the Trail Smoke Eaters at the 1963 IIHF World Championships, but his case was turned down. It took the arrival of Emile Francis as g.m./coach of the Rangers in 1964 to get the suspension lifted.

"Any brilliant player is helpful to his team, but Maurice [Richard] is something special. Frequently, when things would go wrong on the ice, he would personally rally his faltering mates. Eventually, he would score one of his cataclysmic goals, completely turning the trend of play in favour of his team and ultimate victory."

— Frank Selke Sr., 1962

No one who has ever skated in the NHL played the game with more enthusiasm and emotion than Maurice "Rocket" Richard. That intensity was an answer to former Montreal general manager Tommy Gorman, who called him too brittle and too fragile to ever make it in the NHL. In three successive seasons, he suffered season-ending injuries to his right ankle, wrist and left ankle. After the third injury, Gorman removed Richard's name from the Canadiens' reserve list, but no other team claimed him. It was Dick Irvin who convinced the Habs to give Richard another chance. When he finally did make it to the NHL to stay, he fiercely protected himself.

" (Maurice Richard) was as good as there was at that time. He had more key goals in more important games then any man ... But he wasn't a fiery person in the dressing room. He saved it all for the ice. He led by example."

— Tom Johnson

" The longest ovation I've ever heard was the ovation for Maurice Richard the night of the closing (of the Montreal Forum). That's the first time I've ever seen tears in his eyes."

— Tom Johnson

" (The ovation at the closing of the Forum) was unbelievable. I felt funny on the ice. I didn't know what to think and it made me cry a little bit, no doubt about that. Six, seven minute ovation. I never had that it my life. I never thought it was going to happen."

— Maurice Richard

" His eyes had fire in them. And the tougher the game got, the more fire there was. Just like coals you see in a barbeque ... His concentration was just incredible and his desire around the net, there was nobody quite like him."

— Bob Baun

Dick Duff may have got behind Jacques Plante *on this night, but that was about the only thing Toronto put past him as Jake the Snake and his Canadiens teammates downed the Leafs 5-2 on February 12, 1958.*

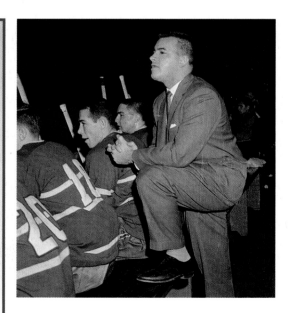

"(Anywhere) you could go in Montreal, whether you were English or French it didn't matter, the Canadiens were the fans' team. And you know, you were sort of the guardian or the custodian and you better not lose the keys."

— Scotty Bowman

Pollock protege Scotty Bowman *worked his way up through the Canadiens' junior and minor-league affiliates. His first NHL coaching job was with the expansion St. Louis Blues in 1967-68, but in 1971-72 he would return to Montreal and lead a talented Habs team to five Stanley Cup championships in eight seasons behind the bench.*

> " *Toe Blake has to go down as one of the greatest coaches of all time. As for motivating players, I don't think there ever has been or will be a greater coach than Toe Blake in that regard."*
>
> — Sam Pollock.

> " *I think that if we had a Toe Blake behind the bench and Punch [Imlach] as a general manager, nobody would have come close to what we could have done."*
>
> — Bob Baun

With each of his four raised fingers *representing a consecutive Stanley Cup championship, coach Toe Blake celebrates the Canadiens' 5-3 decision over the Toronto Maple Leafs in the fifth and final game of the 1959 Stanley Cup finals. Sharing the spotlight is forward Marcel Bonin, whose goal at 9:55 of the second period proved to be the Cup-winner. By defeating the Leafs, Blake and the Habs also eclipsed Toronto's record of three consecutive Cup wins.*

With his eyes still displaying their intimidating "red" glare, *Rocket Richard deposits the final goal of his storied NHL career behind Johnny Bower during game three of the 1960 Stanley Cup finals. Tim Horton, Allan Stanley, Henri Richard, Dickie Moore and Gerry Ehman were the on-ice observers to this moment of NHL history. Richard reported to training camp the following September, but retired before the season began.*

Johnny Bower stops a chest-high shot off the stick of "Pocket Rocket" Richard as Tim Horton, Allan Stanley and Maurice Richard look on during the 1960 Stanley Cup finals. When the Rocket told the Canadiens brass that his baby brother "was ready" for the big time just before the start of the 1955-56 season, the Habs immediately signed the youngster to a three-year contract.

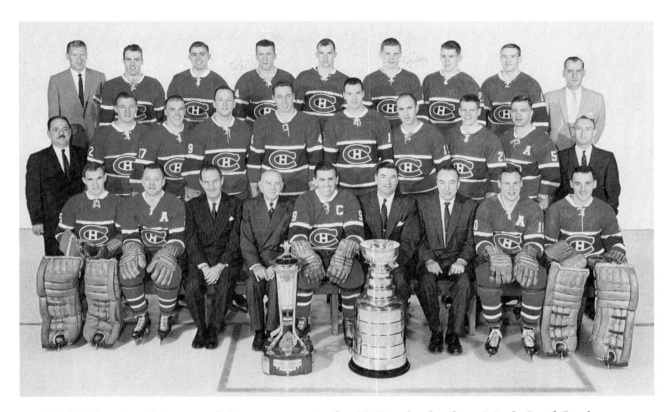

This Montreal team picture was part of a 1961 calender from Maple Leaf Gardens that featured a tribute to the 1960 Stanley Cup champion Canadiens, who swept the Leafs in the 1960 finals with four one-sided victories. Only four of the players featured on this calendar would play their entire NHL careers with the Habs: Maurice Richard, front row, centre; Jean Béliveau, second row, fifth from left; Henri Richard, back row, second from left; and Claude Provost, back row, fourth from left. These big wall calenders, brimming with full colour photos of NHL and minor-league award winners and winning teams, were a prized commodity. The calenders were distributed to barber shops across Canada, leaving many dedicated fans begging their barber for possession of the keepsake.

NHL president Clarence Campbell is flanked by Jacques Plante, left, and Maurice Richard following the Canadiens' fifth straight Stanley Cup victory, a four-game sweep of the Maple Leafs. With their stable lineup—eleven players were with the team for all five Cup wins—explosive offense and suffocating defense, the Canadiens lost only nine playoff games during their five-year reign as Stanley Cup champions.

Conn Smythe addresses a distinguished hockey crowd *at the official opening of the old Hockey Hall of Fame on the grounds of Toronto's Canadian National Exhibition in 1961. Each NHL captain raised his team's flag to mark the opening. Note Béliveau and Armstrong, poised to get their team's flag up the pole first (see below). Other dignitaries in attendance included Canadian prime Minister John Diefenbaker and an array of pioneer hockey superstars including Cyclone Taylor.*

“

I'll tell you one thing about the rivalry that went on when they opened the old Hockey Hall of Fame in 1961. There were six flagpoles out front. Each team had been asked to design a flag representing its team colours. They had a few speeches and all the team captains were there to run their flags up the pole when the Hall was declared officially open. I remember Selke telling Béliveau, 'I know those Leafs. You get your flag ready and don't wait. We want our flag to be up there first.' And sure enough, Toronto had a little thing going that they were going to raise their flag first, but we were just a little bit ahead of them and raised our Canadiens flag up first. The rivalry ran through everything.”

— Ken Reardon

FOREVER
RIVALS
1960 • 1979

George Armstrong manoeuvers into the slot *to snare a loose puck under the watchful glare of Jean-Guy Talbot (17), J.C. Tremblay (3) and Jacques Plante during the 1960-61 season. The Canadiens had a policy of pairing rookie defensemen with veterans who played a similar style. Tremblay learned his lessons well from his partner, and went on to play in the NHL and WHA until 1979.*

Coach Imlach delivers a punch line to friend, assistant and goodwill ambassador King Clancy. With his ever-present smile, astute observations and gift of gab, Clancy was a irreplaceable member of the Leafs' organization for over fifty years.

" [Punch Imlach] was a gambler. He knew how far to go with a certain player and how far not to go and he played all kinds of little games. I don't think that he was that great for my talents. I think I would have done better somewhere else."

— Frank Mahovlich

1961-62 ✦ TORONTO MAPLE LEAFS ✦ 1961-62

WORLD CHAMPIONS AND STANLEY CUP WINNERS

The Stanley Cup portrait of the 1961-62 Maple Leafs still prominently featured team founder Conn Smythe, even though he was no longer an operating partner. In November 1961, Smythe surrendered control of the franchise to a triumvirate that included his son Stafford, Harold Ballard and media magnate John Bassett. By 1971, Stafford Smythe was dead, Bassett was out of the picture and Ballard was in jail.

Using an efficient combination of aggressiveness and clean play, Dave Keon played more than two decades in the NHL and WHA. Although he was a dynamo on the ice and constantly in his opponents' face, Keon spent less than 10 minutes in the penalty box in 14 of his 18 years in the league.

Any team coached by Punch Imlach was guaranteed to have a leg up on the opposition. Two members of the 1961-62 championship club, Ed Litzenberger (third from left) and Al Arbour (fourth from left) were also members of the 1961 champion Chicago Black Hawks. Until Claude Lemieux turned the trick in 1996, they were the last two players to win consecutive championships with different teams.

Gilles Tremblay (21) drills a shot past Johnny Bower during game four of the 1963 semi-final series between the Leafs and Canadiens. Tremblay's goal kept the Habs alive, but the Leafs quickly turned out the lights on the Canadiens with a 5-0 victory in the fifth game of the best-of-seven set.

For much of the 1960s, Don Cherry *was the property of the Toronto Maple Leafs, but with an all-star defense corps ahead of him, Cherry couldn't crack the Leafs' NHL line-up. While in the Leafs' organization, Cherry played on three AHL Calder Cup championship teams in Rochester. During his 17-year career, Cherry patrolled the blueline in Hershey, Boston, Springfield, Trois Rivières, Kitchener-Waterloo, Sudbury, Spokane, Rochester, Tulsa and Vancouver.*

Billy Harris, left, and Ron Stewart administer a champagne shower to *Stanley Cup hero Bobby Baun following Toronto's 4-0 whitewashing of the Detroit Red Wings in game seven of the 1964 finals. Baun's heroics came during game six in Detroit. With the Leafs trailing 3-2 in the series and the match knotted at 3-3 in the final frame, Baun blocked a shot with his foot, and immediately fell to the ice in pain. Unable to leave the ice under his own steam, a stretcher was summoned and Baun was carried into the Olympia clinic. While it was clear to both Baun and Leaf trainer Bobby Haggert that Baun had broken a bone in his ankle, Baun refused to leave the game. He returned to the bench just as overtime was beginning and was on the ice a minute later when he intercepted a Wing clearing pass at the blueline and flipped a shot toward the Red Wing net. The puck bounced off Wing blueliner Bill Gadsby and past a shocked Terry Sawchuk to give Toronto a 4-3 win. Two nights later, with his ankle tightly wrapped, Baun took a regular shift as the Leafs won their third consecutive Stanley Cup championship.*

"*I didn't know much of anything at [the time I broke my leg]. It was an emotional time for me. I'd had a good year going, so I was really motivated and I was having a good time and enjoying what I was doing. It was interesting when it happened. I went off and I asked the doctor, I said 'What can we do?' And he said, 'Well, we can tape it and freeze it and see what happens.' So we did. I scored the goal almost immediately when I went out on the ice, so I really didn't have much time to try [the leg] out, to know what was going to happen."*

— Bob Baun

Carl Brewer always marched to the beat of his own drummer, and nothing riled Punch Imlach more than a player who practiced individualism in a team setting. That led to numerous office battles between Brewer and Imlach, eventually causing the three-time All-Star to retire before the 1965-66 season. Brewer went on to regain his amateur status so he could join the Canadian National Team. He later went on to play in Detroit, St. Louis and the WHA before moving to Finland to help coach the Finnish National Team. Incredibly, after six seasons on the sidelines and 14 years after walking out of training camp in 1965, Brewer returned to play for Imlach and the Leafs at the age of 41 in 1979-80.

The 1963-64 Maple Leafs bear more than a passing similarity to the 1948-49
*version of the club. Both defending championship teams were struggling merely to
get a ticket to the post-season dance. And like Conn Smythe before him, Punch
Imlach needed a playmaking centre to revitalize the Leaf attack. On February 22, he
swung a five-for-two deal with the Rangers that brought Andy Bathgate
and Don McKenney to the Leafs for a quintet of talented players. Bathgate, shown
here, got to raise the Cup above his head two months later, but both he and
McKenney were wearing Detroit colours fourteen months later. The five men
Imlach surrendered for one more swig of Stanley Cup champagne— Bob Nevin, Bill
Collins, Dick Duff, Arnie Brown and Rod Seiling—went on to play a combined 61
seasons in the league after leaving the Leafs.*

Following the 1964 finals, a group of sportswriters and coaches gathered to select an "unofficial" most valuable player for the playoffs. Bob Pulford, who was a tower of strength throughout the post-season, edged out Gordie Howe by a single point (7-6) to win the first playoff MVP award. NHL president Clarence Campbell admitted the idea of establishing a permanent trophy to honor the playoff MVP was an intriguing one but said, "nothing has been decided. Several names have been forwarded, including those of Conn Smythe, Lester Patrick and Bill Barilko." The following year, the Conn Smythe Trophy was introduced for presentation to the top performer in the post-season.

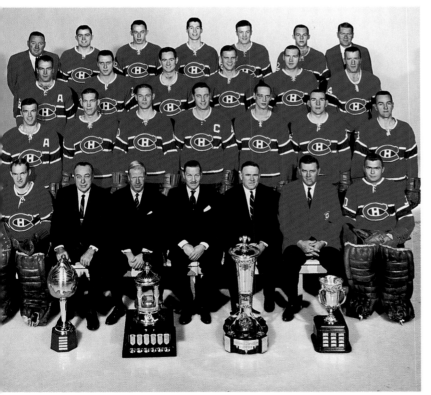

The 1963-64 Montreal Canadiens collected a load of silverware, including the Vezina Trophy (Charlie Hodge), Hart Trophy (Jean Béliveau), Calder Trophy (Jacques Laperriere) and the Prince of Wales Trophy (first place overall), but the biggest prize of all was snatched from their grasp by the Toronto Maple Leafs. The goaltender at the far right of the bottom row is Gary Bauman, who didn't appear in a game with Montreal until the 1966-67 season when Gump Worsley went down with a knee injury. A graduate of Michigan Tech University, Bauman was the first collegiate goaltender to play for the Canadiens.

Rompin' Ronnie Ellis *(8) sidesteps a sprawled Gump Worsley with Terry Harper closing ground during Leafs/Habs action in the 1965-66 season. A frustrated Ellis retired following the 1974-75 season after seeing much of the Leafs' talent defect to the WHA. Brad Selwood, Rick Ley, Norm Ullman, Dave Keon, Bernie Parent and Blaine Stoughton were just six of the 18 Leafs to jump ship because Harold Ballard refused to match salaries with the fledgling league. When Roger Neilson came aboard for the 1977-78 season, Ellis returned to the Leafs fold and compiled 26 goals and 24 assists in 80 games.*

***Tim Horton (7), Allan Stanley (26) and Red Kelly
(4)*** *surround goaltender Johnny Bower as Canadiens' players Claude Larose (11) and Ralph Backstrom (6) attack the
Leafs net during action in the 1965-66 season. Chicago
owner Jim Norris once offered Frank Selke $135,000 for the
services of Backstrom, but the crafty Montreal g.m. cried
foul, replying, "Jim, whenever a player comes along who is
worth that price, his place is in the Canadiens' lineup."*

Eddie Shack *wheels away from his main adversary, John Ferguson, as rookie netminder Gary Smith looks on during the 1965-66 season. Smith wasn't yet tabbed with the moniker "Suitcase", but by the time his career came to an end in 1980, he had donned the jerseys of seven different NHL teams and two WHA clubs.*

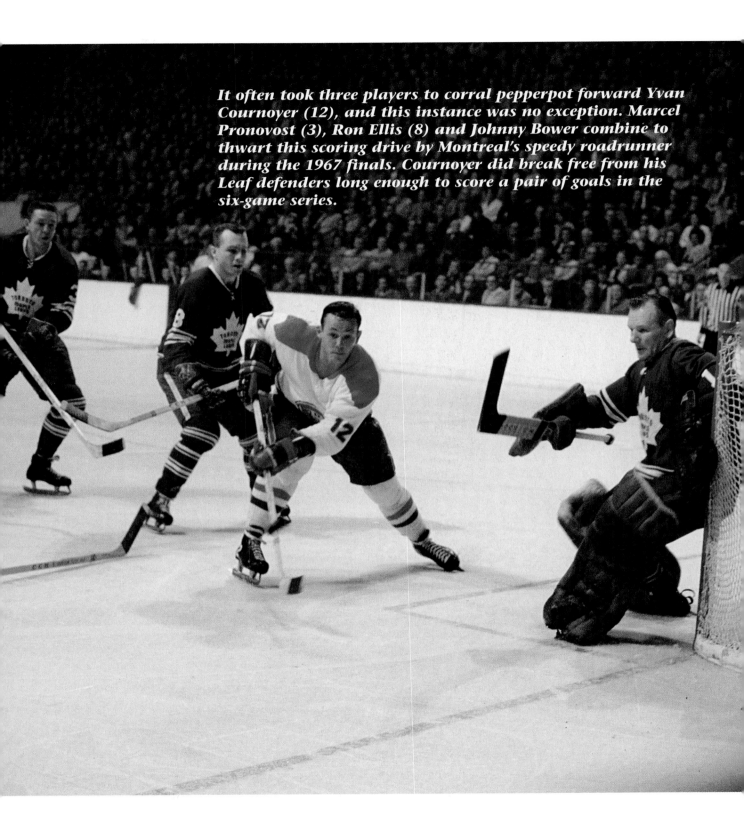

It often took three players to corral pepperpot forward Yvan Cournoyer (12), and this instance was no exception. Marcel Pronovost (3), Ron Ellis (8) and Johnny Bower combine to thwart this scoring drive by Montreal's speedy roadrunner during the 1967 finals. Cournoyer did break free from his Leaf defenders long enough to score a pair of goals in the six-game series.

Terry Sawchuk escapes the grasp *of Montreal forechecker Claude Provost, while Allan Stanley strains to keep up during action in the 1967 Stanley Cup finals. The Habs were expected to easily defeat the overage wonders from Toronto, but Sawchuk was exceptional in goal, providing NHL fans with one last glimpse of his greatness. Although he promised he would retire after the series, he found that he couldn't live without the game. He went on to play with Los Angeles, Detroit and the New York Rangers.*

Jean Béliveau pursues Tim Horton *behind the Leaf net during the sixth and deciding game of the Stanley Cup finals in 1967, Canada's Centennial Year. The Leafs changed their uniform crest for the 1967 playoffs, donning the solid eleven-point maple leaf shown here. This maple leaf was similar in design to the one on the new Canadian flag that was adopted in 1965.*

Pete Stemkowski (12), Jim Pappin (18) and Tim Horton (7) *celebrate Pappin's goal in game six of the 1967 Stanley Cup final. Pappin, the leading scorer in the playoffs, sent a cross-ice pass toward Stemkowski that deflected off Montreal defender Terry Harper's skate past a bewildered Gump Worsley. It turned out to be the Stanley Cup-winning goal.*

A group of proud old pappies –
*Johnny Bower (42), Marcel Pronovost
(36), George Armstrong (36), Red Kelly
(39), Terry Sawchuk (37) and Allan
Stanley (41) – surround coach Punch
Imlach and Lord Stanley's proud old Mug
on May 5, 1967. All seven men would
eventually be inducted into the Hockey
Hall of Fame, but none of them would
ever see his name etched on the silver
barrel of the Stanley Cup again.*

Bernie Parent, seen here wearing a mask designed by Jacques Plante, joined the Leafs on February 2, 1971 in a trade that sent Mike Walton and Bruce Gamble to the Flyers. Parent's stay in Toronto was brief and he became the first established NHL player to sign with the newly formed World Hockey Association when he inked a contract with the Miami Screaming Eagles in March, 1972.

The first defenseman to win the Conn
Smythe Trophy as playoff MVP in
1969, Serge Savard would prove to be a
mainstay along the Montreal blueline
for 14 seasons. A flashy skater until a
badly broken leg slowed him down,
Savard was a rock in his own zone and
one of the best ever at moving players
from in front of the net.

Yvan "The Roadrunner" Cournoyer (12) slams on the brakes to avoid a collision with Guy Trottier (11), Guy Charron (23) and Jacques Plante during Toronto's 6-2 romp over the Canadiens on October 28, 1970. Cournoyer began his career as a special teams player— 20 of his 25 goals in the 1966-67 season were scored on the powerplay—but quickly evolved into a versatile forechecker and deadly sniper from the right side.

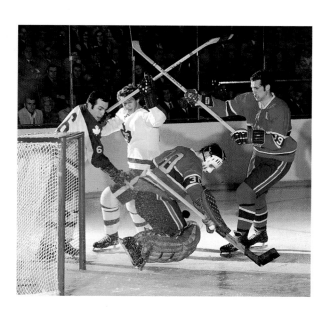

Ron Ellis digs at Rogie Vachon's feet for a loose puck while Terry Harper (19) and Darryl Sittler get their sticks up near the Habs crease. Ellis wore #8 when he joined the Leafs in 1964, but Ace Bailey, who was working as an off-ice official at the Gardens, liked Ellis and asked the young winger to wear Bailey's old #6 that had not been used since Ace was injured in December 1933. Ellis accepted Bailey's offer and wore the number for the remainder of his career.

For the last time in his illustrious career, *Jean Béliveau hoists the Stanley Cup above his shoulders following the Montreal Canadiens' 3-2 win over Chicago in game seven of the 1971 finals. For one of the few times in their history, the Canadiens were decided underdogs when the playoffs began, but after shocking Boston, outlasting Minnesota and out-smarting Chicago, the Canadiens had their 16th Stanley Cup victory. Perhaps the key game in the entire playoffs came early in their series against Boston. The Bruins took the opening match 3-1 and held a commanding 5-1 lead with 25 minutes left to play in game two. Béliveau, perhaps sensing that his final opportunity to sip Stanley Cup champagne was slipping away, kick-started the comeback with a pair of goals and an assist in the third period as the Habs rebounded for a 7-5 win. Only days after this photo was taken, Béliveau announced his retirement.*

"I think (the 1971 Stanley Cup) would have to go down as one of the greatest, if not the greatest, triumph of the Canadiens. After all, we finished ... maybe 30, 40 points behind Boston ... and we drew them in the first round of the playoffs ... We brought in Ken Dryden, who had only played six games in the league that year, and we beat Boston in seven games in Boston. We then played Minnesota in a very, very hard fought series, and won in six games in Minnesota. And then we played Chicago in the finals — they had a great team with Hull and Mikita — and we beat them in seven games winning the last game in Chicago. So here was a Stanley Cup final where we beat three teams, all on their home ice to win the series."

— Sam Pollock

Part of the appeal of Bob Gainey was his ability to put his words into action on the ice. A cerebral, exacting observer of the game, Gainey was deliberate in his movements on the ice and precise in his analysis of the game off the ice. Gainey transformed the delicate role of the defensive forward into an art form, and the NHL ended up creating a trophy to honour his accomplishments. It's not surprising that Gainey won the Selke Trophy in each of its first four years of presentation.

"I felt more a part of that Stanley Cup [in Montreal in 1971] than any [in Toronto] because I just felt, hey, they gave me more confidence. I was killing penalties, which in 11 years in Toronto I never did. In Montreal, I found myself with my brother, really dominating penalty killing with the Canadiens."

— Frank Mahovlich

Jean Béliveau, whose 500th career goal was set up by Frank Mahovlich, returns the favour by saluting his former teammate's milestone marker on March 21, 1973. Ten years earlier, the very thought of Frank Mahovlich wearing any other uniform, much less the red, white and blue of the Montreal Canadiens, would have been unthinkable. But in January 1971, the Canadiens acquired the Big M, albeit from Detroit. Mahovlich had two contrasting careers during his stay with the Leafs and Canadiens. In Toronto, he was the producer, leading the Leafs in goals in six straight seasons. In Montreal, he was the provider, topping the Habs in assists in each of his three full seasons with the club.

A graduate of the Montreal Jr. Canadiens, Guy Lapointe
spent a year with the Houston Apollos and a season with the
Montreal Voyageurs before being summoned to the NHL by the
Canadiens. Steady defensively and often explosive on offense,
Lapointe became the first - and only - Montreal defenseman in
the history of the franchise to score at least 20 goals in three
consecutive seasons. A four-time All-Star, Lapointe played on
six Stanley Cup-winning teams in Montreal before being dispatched to the St. Louis Blues in 1983.

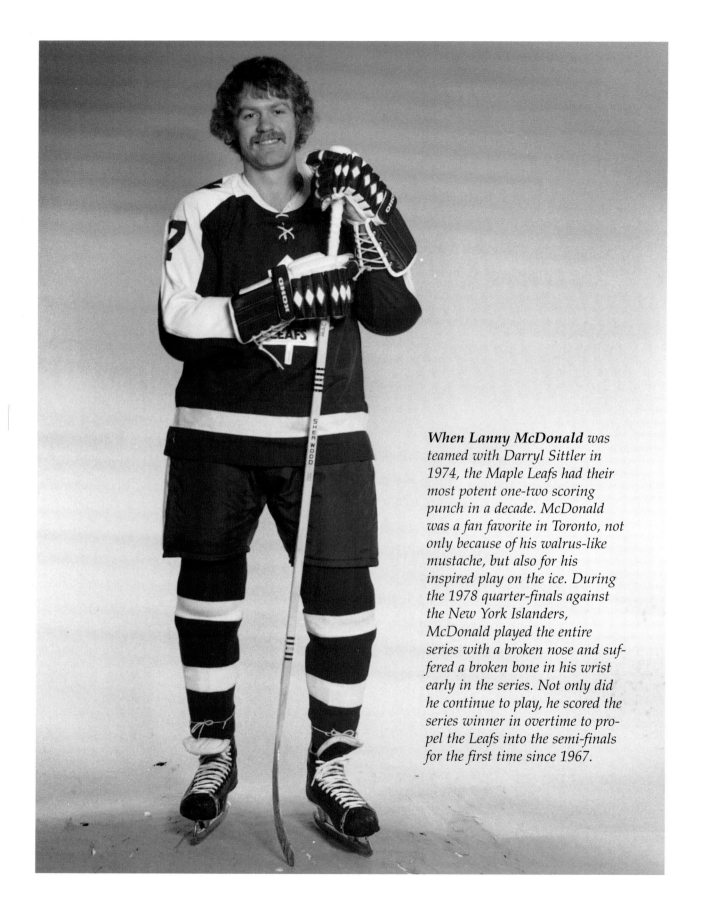

When Lanny McDonald *was teamed with Darryl Sittler in 1974, the Maple Leafs had their most potent one-two scoring punch in a decade. McDonald was a fan favorite in Toronto, not only because of his walrus-like mustache, but also for his inspired play on the ice. During the 1978 quarter-finals against the New York Islanders, McDonald played the entire series with a broken nose and suffered a broken bone in his wrist early in the series. Not only did he continue to play, he scored the series winner in overtime to propel the Leafs into the semi-finals for the first time since 1967.*

During the 1970s, general manager Jim Gregory built the Leafs back into playoff contenders with wise draft selections and astute trades. One draft choice who turned out to be a pleasant surprise was PEI-native Errol Thompson, who, unlike many other Maritime stars, decided to remain in Charlottetown to play junior. Gregory selected him in the second round of the 1970 Amateur Draft, and Thompson responded by earning a full-time berth on the Leafs in 1972-73. Thompson, who played a line with Darryl Sittler and Lanny McDonald, had his finest season in 1975-76 when he scored 43 goals.

Borje Salming's defense partner during much of the 1970s was Ian Turnbull, an offensively gifted rearguard on the ice but wildly unpredictable outside the rink. Turnbull's finest moment in a Leaf uniform came on February 2, 1977, when he became the first and only defenseman in NHL history to score five goals in a single game. He was a personal favourite of owner Harold Ballard, who once declared, "I wouldn't trade Ian Turnbull for God," which prompted one Toronto scribe to retort, "How about God and a first-round draft choice?"

Guy Lapointe (5), Jacques Laperriere (2) and Ken Dryden watch closely as Frank Mahovlich clears a rebound from the clutches of Leaf captain Dave Keon. Mahovlich was a changed player after being dealt to Detroit late in the 1967-68 season. He was allowed to go out and play hockey without carrying the weight of a franchise on his back. When he was traded to Montreal in January, 1971, he was unsure he wanted to report, but the chance to play along side his brother Peter finally convinced him to give the Habs a chance.

Every team passed over Larry Robinson in the 1971 Amateur Draft before the Canadiens made him their fourth selection behind Guy Lafleur, Chuck Arnason and Murray Wilson. The "Big Bird," seen here slamming Clark Gillies into the end boards during the 1978 All-Star Game, wasn't even expected to crack the Canadiens lineup. After 112 games in the minors, Robinson arrived in the NHL and went on to become the first NHL player since Stan Mikita to play 20 seasons in the league.

Guy Lafleur poses in front of his trophy case with three miniature Stanley Cups awarded to him and his teammates during the second great Habs dynasty. The Canadiens managed to win the 1973 championship without much of a contribution from Lafleur, but he compensated for that effort with 24 points in the next 19 games he played in the finals during the 1970s.

FOREVER
RIVALS
1980 • 1997

Before he left the Canadiens' organization in 1997, *Sam Pollock acquired the Colorado Rockies' first round selection in the 1980 Entry Draft, a draft that would feature Denis Savard, a Quebec native and a member of the Montreal Jr. Canadiens' legendary "Trois Denis" line with Denis Cyr and Denis Tremblay. As fate would have it, that pick turned out to be the first overall selection. However, instead of choosing the native son, the Canadiens opted for Regina native Doug Wickenheiser, the consensus #1 pick. Wickenheiser could never get untracked in Montreal and lasted less than four seasons with the Canadiens.*

The Montreal Canadiens organization has always been able to find forwards who relished their defensive roles. Guy Carbonneau was not only the Canadiens' finest special teams performer, he was also a valued offensive contributor, scoring at least 20 goals in five of his first nine full seasons with the club.

In his second coming as general manager, Punch Imlach dismantled the team that Jim Gregory had spent a decade assembling. While many of Imlach's moves were questionable, he did swing one trade that paid dividends for the Leafs. In February 1980, he sent Tiger Williams and Jerry Butler to Vancouver for Bill Derlago and Rick Vaive. Derlago, a highly touted prospect who scored 96 goals in junior for Brandon in 1976-77, was the fourth player selected in the 1978 Amateur Draft. He scored at least 30 goals in four of his five full seasons with the Leafs before being traded to Boston in October 1985.

Derlago's partner on right wing was Rick Vaive, *a natural goal scorer who still holds the team record for goals in a season (54) and most 50-goal campaigns (3). Vaive was blessed with a blistering slapshot and a high tolerance for pain, which allowed him to station himself in the slot and take the punishment that accompanies the position. Vaive is currently the coach and general manager of the South Carolina Stingrays in the East Coast Hockey League.*

The Senator in his chambers. *Serge Savard showed his talents were not restricted to the ice surface when he was named the general manager of the Montreal Canadiens on April 28, 1983, only two weeks after the Canadiens were swept out of the playoffs by the Buffalo Sabres. Savard overcame the bitter retirement of Guy Lafleur and career-ending injuries to Pierre Mondou and Mario Tremblay to build the Canadiens into Stanley Cup champions in 1986. The Habs reached the finals three times and won a pair of championships during his 13-year term in office.*

Mats Naslund was the first European-trained player to join the Montreal Canadiens, but in many ways his style and abilities were perfectly molded for a career with the Habs. Small, speedy and smart, Naslund endeared himself to the Montreal fans with his spirited play and spectacular goals.

All three of the Maple Leafs' top picks in the 1984 Entry Draft—Al Iafrate, Todd Gill and Jeff Reese—went on to play for the club. Reese played parts of five seasons with the Leafs, but could never nail down the #1 goaltending job. Traded to Calgary in the deal that brought Doug Gilmour to Toronto, Reese set an NHL record with three assists in the Flames' 13-1 win over San Jose on February 10, 1993.

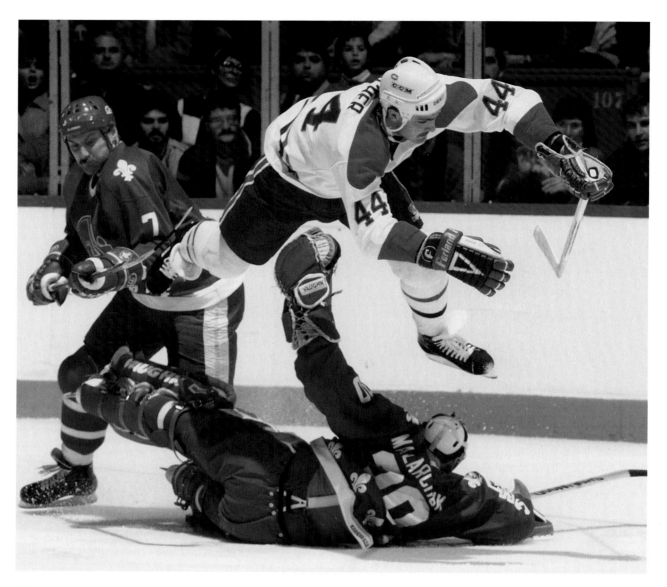

From the moment Guy Lafleur hung up the blades in 1984, the Montreal fans were searching for a player to replace the Lafleur magic. For a short time, they found him in Stephane Richer (44), who became the only other Canadiens player to reach the 50-goal plateau twice. Despite that success, Richer could never convince the fans or management that he was giving his full effort and he was traded to New Jersey only one season after scoring a career-high 51 goals for the Canadiens.

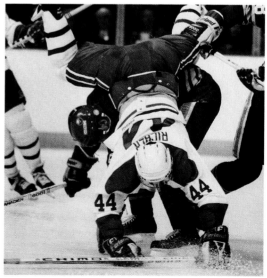

When Conn Smythe was building the Maple Leafs *in the formative days of the franchise, he wanted players who were "tough, but clean." No modern-era player epitomized that adage more than Wendel Clark, a farm boy from Saskatchewan who was a fan favorite at Maple Leaf Gardens from the first moment he stepped on the ice. With his bone-crushing hits and fast fists, Clark gave the Leafs the intimidating force the team had been missing ever since Tiger Williams was traded to Vancouver.*

Like their future teammate Wendel Clark, Russ Courtnall, left, and Gary Leeman, below, had developed their skills with the Hounds of Notre Dame College in Wilcox, Saskatchewan. When the trio were reunited in the NHL with the Maple Leafs, the "Hound Line" was born. Courtnall played for the Canadian Olympic Team in 1984 and joined the Leafs immediately following the Games. Leeman was a natural defenseman who was named as the WHL's top rearguard in 1982-83. When he arrived in the NHL, the Leafs transformed him into a right winger. Leeman improved his offensive totals in each of his first seven seasons with the Leafs, eventually becoming only the second Leaf player to score 50 goals in a season. Both Courtnall and Leeman would later play for the Canadiens.

As a 21-year veteran of the old Eastern Hockey League, *John Brophy was one of the wildest men in hockey's wildest league. When he was given the task of coaching the Toronto Maple Leafs in 1986, he brought that same fiery personality with him when he stepped behind the bench. For a time, it sparked the Leafs, and they came within a single game of advancing to the semifinals in 1986-87. However, Brophy's act soon wore thin, and he was dismissed as coach of the team midway through the 1988-89 season.*

Al Iafrate *was the Maple Leafs' top selection in the 1984 Entry Draft and despite having only ten games of major junior experience, he made the lineup in the 1984-85 season. A gifted offensive performer, Iafrate is the only Leaf defenseman other than Ian Turnbull to twice reach the 20-goal plateau.*

When the Chicago Blackhawks signed Gary Nylund as a free agent in 1986, the Maple Leafs wanted Ed Olczyk, above, as compensation. An arbitrator did not agree with the Leaf request, but Toronto's interest in Olczyk never waned. In September 1987, they finally got their man, sending Rick Vaive, Steve Thomas and Bob McGill to the Windy City for Olczyk and Al Secord. In the 1989-90 season, Olczyk tied a team record with points in 18 straight games, spearheading an aggressive Leaf attack that saw the team finish second in the NHL in goals scored.

Another of Serge Savard's early moves was to sign Brian Skrudland (39), who went undrafted despite collecting 94 points in his final year of junior with the Saskatoon Blades. A tireless worker and a skilled penalty-killer, Skrudland set an NHL record with his first ever playoff goal when he scored after just nine seconds of overtime in game two of the 1986 Stanley Cup finals.

Ryan Walter spent the first four seasons of his career with the Washington Capitals, where post-season success was measured game by game. When he arrived in Montreal as part of the blockbuster deal that sent Rod Langway to Washington, Walter soon learned that nothing short of a Stanley Cup title was accepted. When the Habs were swept by Buffalo in his first playoff series as a Canadien, so many people stopped him on the street demanding an explanation that he had to leave town. In his final season with the Habs, he passed his 1986 Stanley Cup ring around to the younger players, so they would realize that in Montreal, winning isn't everything, it's the only thing.

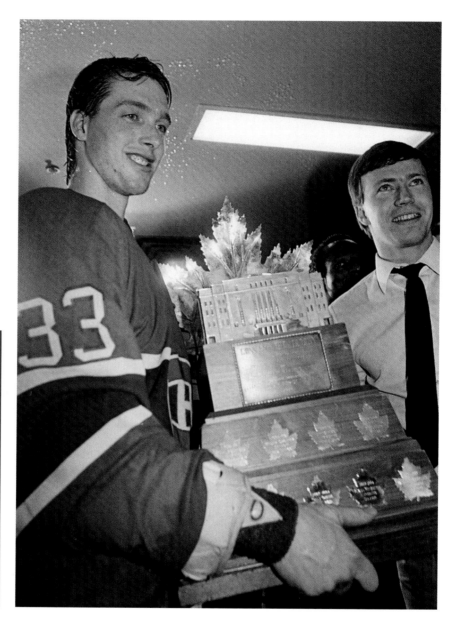

Although he had guided the Sherbrooke Canadiens to the AHL championship in 1985, Patrick Roy was better known for his idiosyncratic on-ice behavior than his sterling play between the pipes. The 21-year old rookie would crane his neck like a prehistoric bird and carry on animated conversations with his goal-posts as part of his pre-game ritual, but once play was under way, he was all business. Despite leading all rookie goaltenders in wins (23) and goals-against average (3.35) in the 1985-86 season, the best was yet to come for the freshman netminder. In the 1986 playoffs, Roy led a rookie-laden Canadiens team past Boston, Hartford, the NY Rangers and Calgary as the Habs went on to record the franchise's 23rd Stanley Cup title.

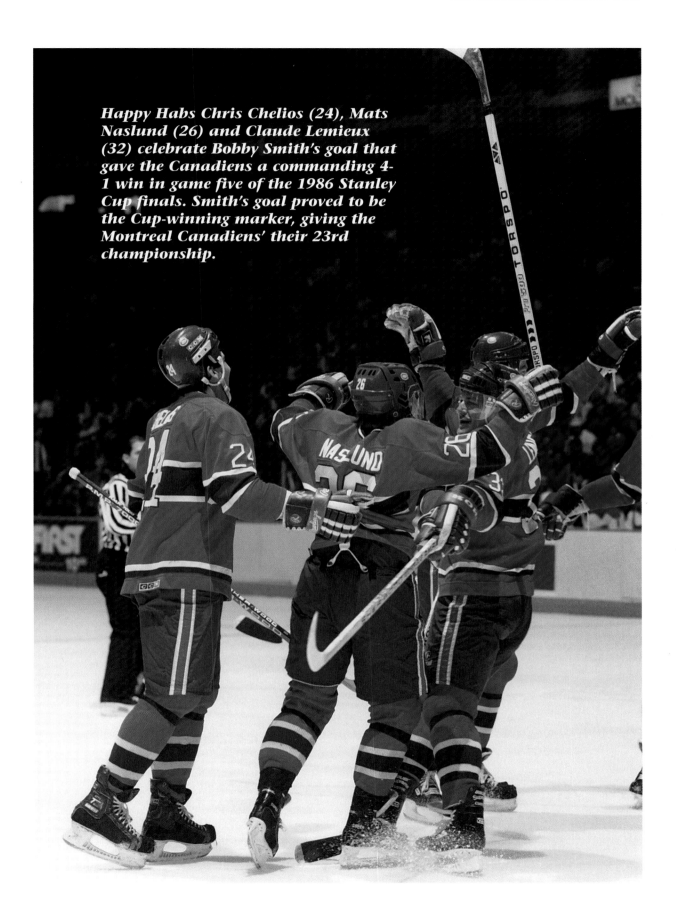

Happy Habs Chris Chelios (24), Mats Naslund (26) and Claude Lemieux (32) celebrate Bobby Smith's goal that gave the Canadiens a commanding 4-1 win in game five of the 1986 Stanley Cup finals. Smith's goal proved to be the Cup-winning marker, giving the Montreal Canadiens' their 23rd championship.

One of the enduring features of the Montreal Canadiens'
franchise has been the ability to scout and sign outstanding
defensive prospects. In the 1981 Entry Draft, the Canadiens
used their fifth choice to select a young rearguard named
Chris Chelios from the Moose Jaw Canucks. A native of
Chicago, Chelios was a U.S. Olympian and a collegiate all-
star with the University of Wisconsin Badgers before joining
the Canadiens following the 1984 Winter Games. One of the
rare defenseman to never spend a minute in the minors,
Chelios quickly adapted to the NHL game, winning a berth on
the All-Rookie Team in 1985 before winning the Norris
Trophy as the league's top blueliner in 1989.

During the 1988-89 season, *coach John Brophy demanded that Russ Courtnall—whom he considered too soft to play on "his" team—be traded for some muscle. Rookie g.m. Gord Stellick was left with little choice, so he unloaded Courtnall to Montreal in return for John Kordic, a loose cannon on skates. While Kordic may have excited the fans, his unruly behaviour off the ice made him a liability. After 104 games with the Leafs, Kordic and Paul Fenton were dispatched to Washington for a fifth-round draft selection.*

Maybe you can **go home again.** On June 29, 1990, after 10 seasons with the Chicago Blackhawks, Denis Savard returned to Montreal, where he had been a sensation as a junior. Although he showed signs of brilliance, he didn't dazzle the denizens in the Forum like he did in Chicago Stadium. Then again, the Blackhawks never reached the finals during his decade with the team, whereas the Canadiens rolled into the championship round in his third season. Ironically, just as he was preparing to play in his first Stanley Cup final, he suffered a broken foot and had to watch his teammates win the championship from the sidelines.

Since joining the Leafs in November 1990, Dave Ellett has been one of the Leafs' steadiest defensemen. In the 1993 playoffs, he set a club record for defensemen with 18 post-season points.

When the Calgary Flames advanced to the championship finals in 1986 and 1989, a key to their success was the team's solid defensive unit constructed by g.m. Cliff Fletcher. One of the integral members of that group was Jamie Macoun, who later followed Cliff Fletcher to Toronto in January 1991. The very fact that Macoun was playing hockey was a testament to his dedication to the game. In the summer of 1987, Macoun suffered severe nerve damage to his arm in a car accident. He missed the entire 1987-88 season, but returned the following season and helped lead the Flames to a Stanley Cup title.

Sylvain Lefebvre spent only two seasons with the Leafs, but the club advanced to the semi-finals in both years, thanks in large part to the defensive system implemented by coach Pat Burns and executed to perfection by Lefebvre. A poised veteran who played under Burns in Montreal, Lefebvre's dedication to defense helped Felix Potvin lead the NHL in goals-against average in his rookie season.

I'm not gonna lie. When I play against the Montreal Canadiens, yeah, I want to beat 'em. I want to beat 'em bad."

— Doug Gilmour

Peter Zezel used his skills as a professional soccer player to become one of the NHL's top face-off men. When he's taking a draw, Zezel will often tie up the opposing centre, then kick the puck to a teammate. When he was with the Leafs, Zezel often played on a hard working line with Mark Osborne and Bill Berg.

FACING PAGE:
For the first time since the days of Darryl Sittler, the fans in Maple Leaf Gardens had to opportunity to watch a superstar in action when Cliff Fletcher brought Doug Gilmour to Toronto in January of 1991. Most fans were unaware of Gilmour's talent, desire and infectious personality. Within months of arriving in the city, he was Toronto's most popular athlete, a remarkable achievement considering the Blue Jays were winning a pair of World Series Championships just down the road. With Gilmour's gritty work ethic driving the team, the Leafs advanced to the semi-finals in 1993 and 1994, and established an NHL record by winning their first ten games of the 1993-94 season.

Eric Desjardins' star rose to epic proportions in game two of the 1993 Stanley Cup finals between Los Angeles and Montreal. He became the first defenseman in NHL history to score a hat-trick in a Stanley Cup final game. With the Habs already down a game and trailing the second match 2-1 with less than two minutes remaining, coach Jacques Demers called for a measurement on Kings' defenseman Marty McSorley's stick. The lumber was ruled illegal, giving the Canadiens a last-minute powerplay. First Desjardins scored the game-tying goal with 73 ticks left on the clock, then he finished off his three-goal night with the game-winner only 51 seconds into overtime.

In a "dream-come-true-moment" native-son Denis Savard finally gets to celebrate his Stanley Cup moment in Montreal. The Canadiens, who had a long tradition of drafting the top Quebec-born talent, bypassed Savard in the 1980 Entry Draft to select a rangy winger from Regina named Doug Wickenheiser. In 1990, the Habs sent all-star defenseman Chris Chelios to Chicago for Savard, and he helped guide the Canadiens to another Stanley Cup title in 1993, although a foot injury forced him to the sidelines in the finals.

Of all the players to wear the Maple Leaf, *few have suffered the wrath of the fans more than defenseman Todd Gill. Costly mental errors and ill-timed giveaways plagued Gill throughout his career, yet he survived longer than the three general managers, seven coaches, four captains and countless teammates that passed through town during his 12 seasons with the club. When Pat Burns assumed Toronto's coaching duties, he showed great confidence in Gill and his abilities. Gill responded by playing the best hockey of his career. His tenure as the longest-serving Leaf since Borje Salming came to an end in June 1996 when he was traded to the San Jose Sharks for defensive specialist Jamie Baker.*

Mike Eastwood battles San Jose defenders *Jayson Moore and Arturs Irbe while Shawn Cronin and Gaetan Duchesne combine to slow down Mike Gartner in game six of the 1993 Western Division quarterfinals. Moments later, Gartner ripped a slapshot past Irbe to give the Leafs a 3-2 victory and the tie the series at three games apiece.*

Saku Koivu became only the second European-born player selected in the first round of the Entry Draft by the Montreal Canadiens when the Habs choose him 21st overall in the 1993 draft. Similar in size and style to Mats Naslund, Koivu impressed the fans at the Forum with his energetic play and break-out speed. One of only three NHL rookies to play all 82 games during the 1995-96 season, Koivu led all Montreal freshmen in scoring with 45 points.

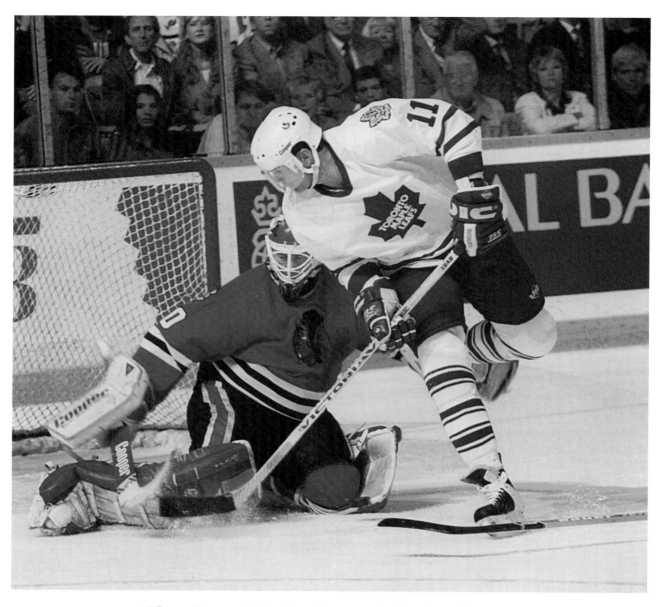

There is an old adage in sports *that "speed never slumps." Mike Gartner, seen here challenging Chicago's Ed Belfour, continues to be one of the game's fastest skaters and one of the NHL's most consistent performers. Gartner is the only player in league history to score 30 goals in 16 different seasons.*

Although many scouts questioned his size and desire, *Valeri Bure proved he could handle the rigors of the NHL game during the 1995-96 season. A two-time WHL West all-star with the Spokane Chiefs, Bure recorded 48 points in 42 games with the AHL's Fredericton Canadiens before making his NHL debut with the parent club midway through the 1994-95 season. In 1995-96, he was teamed with Saku Koivu and Marc Bureau, and the trio became one of the Canadiens' most dynamic forward combinations.*

> *The first time I entered Maple Leaf Gardens, it felt as if I'd died and gne to heaven. You could feel the tradition as you walked the halls and corridors. The air hummed with history."*
>
> — Paul Henderson

Maple Leaf Gardens

Maple Leaf Gardens

> *What a wonderful place to go. The joy of going there, and knowing you're going to play the Montreal Canadiens, knowing that you're going to be at the old Montreal Forum ... You knew it was going to be a hockey game and it didn't matter whether you were sick or you were tired, you went out and you played the game of your life."*
>
> — Carl Brewer

Montreal Forum

Molson Centre

PHOTO CREDITS

Graig Abel: 176, 178; Harold Barkley: front cover, 8, 13, 81, 121; Bruce Bennett Studios: 72, 88, 89, 155, 161, back cover (right); Paul Bereswill: 144; David Bier: 130 (bottom), 160 (top); Michael Burns: 66, 114 (top), 119, 124 (top), 134; Canada Wide: 132, 135 (bottom); Dan Diamond: 74; Dan Diamond & Associates – file photo: 1, 14, 22, 30, 55, 68, 69, 70, 71, 77, 78, 87 (top), 90, 92 (top), 110 (top), 112, 117 (bottom), 120, 135 (top), 145, 147, 148 (top), 149, 151, 154 (bottom), 156, 157, 158, 159, 162, 163, 165 (bottom), 166, 167, 168, 169, 170, 171, 172, 173, 174 (top), 175; Bob Fisher: 91, 165 (top); Hockey Hall of Fame – file photo: 12, 35, 36, 40, 65, 79, 94, 95, 97, 98, 99, 101 (bottom), 118 (top), 123, 125 (top), 148 (bottom); Hockey Hall of Fame – Graphic Artists Collection: iii, 3, 6, 10, 28, 86, 141, 142, 143, 146, 150, 152; Hockey Hall of Fame – Imperial Oil Turofsky Collection: 17, 18, 23, 25, 27, 41, 43, 44, 46, 48, 50, 51, 52, 54, 57, 59, 61, 63, 80, 82, 84, 85, 87 (bottom), 93, 96, 100, 101 (top), 102, 103, 104, 105, 106, 107, 109, 110 (bottom), 111, 113, 114 (bottom), 115 (top), 117 (top), 118 (bottom), 122, 124 (bottom), 125 (bottom), 126, 127, 128, 129, 130 (top), 131, 180 (second from top); Hockey Hall of Fame – Doug MacLellan Collection: 92 (bottom), 172 (inset), 177, 179, back cover (left); Hockey Hall of Fame – Frank Prazak Collection: 2, 4, 7, 9, 20, 26, 49, 83, 116, 133, 136, 137, 138, 139, 140; La Presse: 16, 115 (bottom); Doug MacLellan/The Ice Age: 31, 164; McCord Museum of Canadian History, Notman Photographic Archives: 33; Doug McLatchy Collection: 108 ; Montreal Canadiens: 180 (second from bottom, bottom); Andre Pichette: 174 (bottom); Toronto Maple Leafs: 180 (top); Westfile/Bob Mummery: 76; Bill Wippert: 160 (bottom)

ALL-TIME RECORD
MONTREAL CANADIENS VS. TORONTO MAPLE LEAFS

REGULAR SEASON

OVERALL

GP	MTL. WINS	TOR. WINS	TIES	MTL. GF	TOR. GF	MTL. PTS.	TOR. PTS.
631	304	243	84	1951	1731	692	570

IN MONTREAL

315	192	83	40	1123	776	424	206

IN TORONTO

316	112	160	44	828	955	268	364

PLAYOFFS

SERIES:	MTL. WINS	TOR. WINS	GAMES:	MTL. WINS	TOR. WINS	MTL. GF	TOR. GF
15	8	7	71	42	29	215	160

TOP TEN GAMES
MONTREAL CANADIENS VS. TORONTO MAPLE LEAFS

April 21, 1951 • Toronto 3, Montreal 2 (OT)
Bill Barilko's last NHL goal delivers the Cup to Toronto.

March 23, 1944 • Montreal 5, Toronto 1
Maurice Richard scores all five goals and is named first, second and third star.

May 2, 1967 • Toronto 3, Montreal 1
George Armstrong's empty-net goal seals Leafs' last Cup victory.

April 14, 1960 • Montreal 4, Toronto 0
Canadiens put final flourish on greatest dynasty in NHL history.

April 9, 1964 • Toronto 3, Montreal 1
Dave Keon single-handedly lifts Leafs into Cup finals with three-goal performance.

April 21, 1979 • Montreal 4, Toronto 3 (2OT)
Cam Connors's only playoff goal as a Hab ends double-overtime marathon.

April 13, 1965 • Montreal 4, Toronto 3 (OT)
Claude Provost and the Habs end the Leafs' three-year Stanley Cup reign.

March 31, 1945 • Toronto 3, Montreal 2
Despite finishing 28 points behind Montreal, Leafs bounce Habs from playoffs.

January 9, 1993 • Toronto 5, Montreal 4
Pat Burns's return to Montreal turns new page in Leaf history book.

October 21, 1995 • Montreal 4, Toronto 3
Post-Savard era begins in Montreal with last-second come-from-behind win.

PLAYOFFS
MONTREAL CANADIENS VS. TORONTO MAPLE LEAFS

1918 SEMI-FINALS

Mar.	11	Montreal	3	at	Toronto Arenas	7
Mar.	13	Toronto Arenas	3	at	Montreal	4

Toronto Arenas won two-game, total-goal series 10-7

1925 SEMI-FINALS

Mar.	11	Toronto St. Pats	2	at	Montreal	3
Mar.	13	Montreal	2	at	Toronto St. Pats	0

Montreal won two-game, total-goal series 5-2

1944 SEMI-FINALS

Mar.	21	Toronto	3	at	Montreal	1
Mar.	23	Toronto	1	at	Montreal	5
Mar.	25	Montreal	2	at	Toronto	1
Mar.	28	Montreal	4	at	Toronto	1
Mar.	30	Toronto	0	at	Montreal	11

Montreal won best-of-seven series 4–1

1945 SEMI-FINALS

Mar.	20	Toronto	1	at	Montreal	0	
Mar.	22	Toronto	3	at	Montreal	2	
Mar.	24	Montreal	4	at	Toronto	1	
Mar.	27	Montreal	3	at	Toronto	4	OT (G. Bodnar)
Mar.	29	Toronto	3	at	Montreal	10	
Mar.	31	Montreal	2	at	Toronto	3	

Toronto won best-of-seven series 4–2

1947 FINALS

Apr.	8	Toronto	0	at	Montreal	6	
Apr.	10	Toronto	4	at	Montreal	0	
Apr.	12	Montreal	2	at	Toronto	4	
Apr.	15	Montreal	1	at	Toronto	2	OT (S. Apps)
Apr.	17	Toronto	1	at	Montreal	3	
Apr.	19	Montreal	1	at	Toronto	2	

Toronto won best-of-seven series 4–2

1951 FINALS

Apr.	11	Montreal	2	at	Toronto	3	OT (S. Smith)
Apr.	14	Montreal	3	at	Toronto	2	OT (M. Richard)
Apr.	17	Toronto	2	at	Montreal	1	OT (T. Kennedy)
Apr.	19	Toronto	3	at	Montreal	2	OT (H. Watson)
Apr.	21	Montreal	2	at	Toronto	3	OT (B. Barilko)

Toronto won best-of-seven series 4–1

1959 FINALS

Apr.	9	Toronto	3	at	Montreal	5	
Apr.	11	Toronto	1	at	Montreal	3	
Apr.	14	Montreal	2	at	Toronto	3	OT (D. Duff)
Apr.	16	Montreal	3	at	Toronto	2	
Apr.	18	Toronto	3	at	Montreal	5	

Montreal won best-of-seven series 4–1

1960 FINALS

Apr.	7	Toronto	2	at	Montreal	4
Apr.	9	Toronto	1	at	Montreal	2
Apr.	12	Montreal	5	at	Toronto	2
Apr.	14	Montreal	4	at	Toronto	0

Montreal won best-of-seven series 4–0

1963 SEMI-FINALS

Mar.	26	Montreal	1	at	Toronto	3
Mar.	28	Montreal	2	at	Toronto	3
Mar.	30	Toronto	2	at	Montreal	0
Apr.	2	Toronto	1	at	Montreal	3
Apr.	4	Montreal	0	at	Toronto	5

Toronto won best-of-seven series 4-1

1964 SEMI-FINALS

Mar.	26	Toronto	0	at	Montreal	2
Mar.	28	Toronto	2	at	Montreal	1
Mar.	30	Montreal	3	at	Toronto	2
Apr.	2	Montreal	3	at	Toronto	5
Apr.	4	Toronto	2	at	Montreal	4
Apr.	6	Montreal	0	at	Toronto	3
Apr.	8	Toronto	3	at	Montreal	1

Toronto won best-of-seven series 4-3

1965 SEMI-FINALS

Apr.	1	Toronto	2	at	Montreal	3	
Apr.	3	Toronto	1	at	Montreal	3	
Apr.	6	Montreal	2	at	Toronto	3	OT (D. Keon)
Apr.	8	Montreal	2	at	Toronto	4	
Apr.	10	Toronto	1	at	Montreal	3	
Apr.	13	Montreal	4	at	Toronto	3	OT (C. Provost)

Montreal won best-of-seven series 4–2

1966 SEMI-FINALS

Apr.	7	Toronto	3	at	Montreal	4
Apr.	9	Toronto	0	at	Montreal	2
Apr.	12	Montreal	5	at	Toronto	2
Apr.	14	Montreal	4	at	Toronto	1

Montreal won best-of-seven series 4–0

1967 FINALS

Apr.	20	Toronto	2	at	Montreal	6	
Apr.	22	Toronto	3	at	Montreal	0	
Apr.	25	Montreal	2	at	Toronto	3	OT (B. Pulford)
Apr.	27	Montreal	6	at	Toronto	2	
Apr.	29	Toronto	4	at	Montreal	1	
May	2	Montreal	1	at	Toronto	3	

Toronto won best-of-seven series 4–2

1978 SEMI-FINALS

May	2	Toronto	3	at	Montreal	5
May	4	Toronto	2	at	Montreal	3
May	6	Montreal	6	at	Toronto	1
May	9	Montreal	2	at	Toronto	0

Montreal won best-of-seven series 4–0

1979 QUARTER-FINALS

Apr.	16	Toronto	2	at	Montreal	5	
Apr.	18	Toronto	1	at	Montreal	5	
Apr.	21	Montreal	4	at	Toronto	3	OT (C. Connor)
Apr.	22	Montreal	5	at	Toronto	4	OT (L. Robinson)

Montreal won best-of-seven series 4-0

TOP TEN ALL-TIME SCORERS

MONTREAL CANADIENS AND TORONTO MAPLE LEAFS

MONTREAL CANADIENS
REGULAR SEASON

PLAYER	GP	G	A	Pts	PIM
1. Guy Lafleur	961	518	728	1246	399
2. Jean Beliveau	1125	507	712	1219	1029
3. Henri Richard	1256	358	688	1046	928
4. Maurice Richard	978	544	421	965	1285
5. Larry Robinson	1202	197	686	883	783
6. Yvan Cournoyer	968	428	435	863	255
7. Jacques Lemaire	853	366	469	835	217
8. Steve Shutt	871	408	368	776	410
9. Bernie Georffrion	766	371	388	759	689
10. Elmer Lach	664	215	408	623	478

PLAYOFFS

PLAYER	GP	G	A	Pts	PIM
1. Jean Beliveau	162	79	97	176	211
2. Jacques Lemaire	145	61	78	139	63
3. Larry Robinson	203	25	109	134	211
4. Guy Lafleur	124	57	76	133	67
5. Henri Richard	180	49	80	129	181
6. Yvan Cournoyer	147	64	63	127	47
7. Maurice Richard	133	82	44	126	188
8. Bernie Geoffrion	127	56	59	115	88
9. Steve Shutt	96	50	48	98	65
10. Dickie Moore	112	38	56	94	122

TORONTO MAPLE LEAFS
REGULAR SEASON

PLAYER	GP	G	A	Pts	PIM
1. Darryl Sittler	844	389	527	916	763
2. Dave Keon	1062	365	493	858	75
3. Borje Salming	1099	148	620	768	1292
4. George Armstrong	1187	296	417	713	721
5. Ron Ellis	1034	332	308	640	207
6. Frank Mahovlich	720	296	301	597	782
7. Bob Pulford	947	251	312	563	782
8. Ted Kennedy	696	231	329	560	691
9. Rick Vaive	534	299	238	537	940
10. Norm Ullman	535	166	305	471	160

PLAYOFFS

PLAYER	GP	G	A	Pts	PIM
1. Doug Gilmour	52	17	60	77	90
2. Dave Keon	89	32	35	67	6
3. Darryl Sittler	64	25	40	65	120
4. Ted Kennedy	78	29	31	60	42
5. George Armstrong	110	26	34	60	88
6. Frank Mahovlich	84	24	36	60	135
7. Wendel Clark	73	33	26	59	181
8. Red Kelly	70	17	38	55	16
9. Syl Apps	69	25	28	53	16
10. Bob Pulford	89	25	26	51	126

STANLEY CUP CHAMPIONSHIPS

Montreal Canadiens • 24

1916, 1924, 1930, 1931, 1944, 1946, 1953, 1956, 1957, 1958, 1959, 1960, 1965, 1966, 1968, 1969, 1971, 1973, 1976, 1977, 1978, 1979, 1986, 1993.

STANLEY CUP CHAMPIONSHIPS

Toronto Maple Leafs • 13

1918*, 1922**, 1932, 1942, 1945, 1947, 1948, 1949, 1951, 1962, 1963, 1964, 1967.

* - Toronto Arenas   ** - Toronto St. Pats

INDEX